PRAISE FOR

D1515794

"There's a sweet wistfulness to many   ....
They hearken back to a simpler time, when people played shinny
on backyard rinks. In The Rink, Caddell describes the first
backyard rink he built, as a boy, in the winter of 1963—complete
with bumps and hills—and the rinks he built years later for his
children Jack and Emily. The backyard skating rink is "not gold,
but silver," he writes. "It can't be held in your hand, yet its memory
will remain in your heart for many years. There are days you might
curse it and others you will worship it."

Susan Schwartz, Features Editor, The Montreal Gazette

"Sports aficionados, Andrew Caddell, Dave Stubbs and the late
Philip Caddell, have crafted a delightful collection of short stories
on Canada's national sport. The ten stories in The Goal are,
according to the authors, all true. That may well be, but the skillful
prose of these writers intimates at times a tinge of nostalgic skating
around the real events, putting The Goal on par with the best of
Canadian hockey story-telling, both fiction and non-fiction."

The Ottawa Review of Books

"The stories in the book range from the 1935 Stanley Cup to the
present day. This is a great read. I had trouble putting it down and
completed it in one sitting. I loved Andrew Caddell's anecdotes
about growing up in Montreal West and playing on the outdoor
rinks, the feeling about being in his first championship game and
recalling the bond he formed with teammates like Dugie Ross
more than 50 years ago."

Mike Cohen, The Surburban, Montreal

"This is very much a fan's-eye view of hockey, testifying to the
sport's deep roots in the national psyche and capturing with great
warmth how a love of the game is born and how it gets passed from
one generation to the next."

Ian McGillis, Literary Features Columnist, The Montreal Gazette

"The stories are timeless and are as enjoyable to today's hockey fan just as they were to the hockey fans of the period about which the stories were written. In Andrew's stories we see his personal love of the game through "The Goal" and "The Playoff", the tradition of the back yard/community outdoor hockey rink in so many Canadian towns/cities in "La Patinoire" and "The Rink" and his respect for two true legends of the game in Canada; the late Danny Gallivan in "The Voice" and the late Jean Beliveau in "The Gentleman.""

John Poulter, More Than A Fan sports website

"I have always said that you cannot truly understand a country until you understand the sport it plays most passionately. This, then, is more than a book about hockey—it is about the very soul of Canada."

Roy MacGregor, Globe and Mail Columnist and bestselling author of *Home Team: Fathers, Sons and Hockey* (shortlisted for the Governor General's Literary Award)

"You can feel the cold and hear the cut of skates on a backyard rink -- these stories about one family's love of the game will resonate with anyone who has worshipped a hockey hero or played the game at any level."

Roger Smith, former CTV News correspondent

"As a young immigrant from Vietnam, I would watch the Canadian boys take to the ice every winter. Their energy. passion and teamwork inspired me to believe that Canada was a country where everyone could be part of the "team." Reading The Goal brought back that time for me. Every new immigrant child should read this collection of very enjoyable stories."

Caroline Vu, author of Palawan Story and That Summer in Provincetown

THE GOAL

Stories about

Our National Passion

by

Andrew Caddell,
Dave Stubbs
and Philip Caddell

Copyright © 2015 by Andrew Caddell

Published in Canada by
Deux Voiliers Publishing
www.deuxvoilierspublishing.com

Library and Archives Canada Cataloguing in Publication

Caddell, Andrew, 1952-, author
        The Goal : stories about our national passion /
by Andrew Caddell, Dave Stubbs and Philip Caddell.

ISBN 978-1-928049-42-5 (paperback)
978-1-928049-43-2 (Ingram version)

        1. Hockey--Canada. I. Stubbs, Dave, 1957-,
author II. Caddell, Philip, 1913-, author III. Title.

GV848.4.C3C33 2015   796.9620971
C2015-907730-3

Cover Design - Ian Shaw
Cover Photo - Andrew Caddell
Photo Credits – John Mahoney (Montreal Gazette),
Andrew Caddell and Emily Caddell

Legal deposit – Bibliothèque et Archives nationales du Québec, 2015

The Goal is distributed in Canada by Red Tuque Books (www.redtuquebooks.ca). Use ISBN 978-1-928049-42-5 to order; The Goal is also distributed by Ingram in Canada and world-wide. Use ISBN 978-1-928049-43-2 to order.

To Pip Caddell

This book is dedicated to Philip "Pip" Caddell (1913-2004), who taught his children and grandchildren that sport was similar to life in many ways, as it prepared us for the highs and lows of triumph and defeat—but that doing your best was just as good as winning.

Foreword

The Goal: a book to celebrate Canadians

This book came from a passion for hockey that resides deep in the souls of millions of Canadians.

In my case, it was a passion handed down from two men in my family: my maternal grandfather and my father, who came to Canada from Scotland as a teenager. My grandfather told many stories of playing in arenas in Quebec City in the early 20th century against the likes of Joe Malone and Paddy Moran, two of the early greats of the game. My father, despite never having played hockey, fell in love with the game and followed it all his adult life, becoming part of the passing parade of hockey history, as this book attests.

This book was written for my sons, James and Jack, one who learned to skate on ponds in rural Quebec, and the other who played with Swiss boys who envied him because he had a Montreal Canadiens sweater. And it is for all of us who love the game, everywhere.

Its speed, intensity, complexity and excitement can arouse passions even the least aggressive among us never knew we had. For hockey, in so many ways, reflects who we are as Canadians. It is a team sport, played in the depths of winter, bringing whole communities together to play or watch. At the same time, it relies on individual skill, finesse, patience, stamina and aggressiveness. And yet, it requires clarity and presence of mind too: it is not an easy task to race up the ice with a puck at the end of a stick, trying to decide whether to pass, shoot, or avoid a collision with an oncoming player.

Canadians throughout the decades in all regions, in both official languages and in many more, have shown a love for our game that is equal to or surpasses the love for national sports elsewhere: football (both kinds), cricket, rugby or baseball. Canadians can, and do, spend hours discussing hockey on cold winter days and hot summer nights. No matter how well they play it, or if they ever did, there is something visceral that arouses their interest.

This is not a complex book, or a novel with many plots and twists. Because it is about all of us, it is an unpretentious attempt at describing our "hockey-love." It also seeks to recognize all of those people who made Canadian hockey great: the fans who pay to watch, the kids who played it, the men and women of all ages who support it, the players who never made it. This book is a salute to all of you.

It began with a little story about my own childhood tribulations as a goaltender and grew to a range of other true stories about real people who had the same love for hockey. Along the way, they were joined by yarns from one of the country's best sports feature journalists, Dave Stubbs. His professionalism, presence and crisp style contributed enormously to the finished product.

The stories in this book are all true: they are about real Canadians doing real things, and all along loving their country and their game. There have been many books written about hockey, but very few about ordinary people and their attachment to the game and its heroes. It is a collection of stories about people you might know or knew. It is also about love, respect and growing up.

While they are real stories about real people, they are also allegories about life itself. About

3

trials and tribulation, about determination, kindness, inspiration, excellence, community, fellowship and fairness.

In a world in which so-called "old-fashioned values" are seen as just that, this book reminds us there are still bedrock beliefs that knit us in a tiny strand across this enormous country.

I hope that when you, the reader, read these little vignettes, you will see in them something of yourself, your family and your friends. That is the goal of this book.

Andrew Caddell
November 2015

When every frozen surface becomes a big-league arena, every small-town kid becomes a star.

THE GOAL: a Collection of Stories about Our National Passion

Photo Credits:

Dedication: Philip Caddell (John Mahoney)
The Playoff: page 17 (Emily Caddell)
The Gentleman: page 65 (Andrew Caddell)
The Kid: page 103 (John Mahoney)
La Patinoire: page 109 (Andrew Caddell)
The Rink : page 123 (Andrew Caddell)

All other photos are public domain.

The Goal

By Andrew Caddell

Each winter in Canada, there is a primitive ritual that shapes many young people for the rest of their lives. Not unlike the process that takes place when wolves, hunting in the dead of night, select the weakest from among a herd of deer. It is swift and without warning. It is the dreaded *goalie cull*.

The goalie cull consists of a decision made commonly by a middle-aged adult, normally male, otherwise known as "The Coach". With the sharp eye of a trained anthropologist, he observes a group of seven-year-old boys or girls and decides who can and cannot skate well enough to move at least a few metres in one or another direction. The result is that those players who do not measure up as skaters are put between the metal posts of a hockey goal. They are now goaltenders, goalies, netminders, puck-eaters. A species apart.

They are then ordered to wear the winter "tools of ignorance"—goalie pads that feel like two large dogs have attached themselves to their legs, a chest protector that squeezes the lungs like a vise and a mask that encases the head. And then, after all this body armour has been attached to the young, sensitive and impressionable young child, they are told that they will be the chosen target for pucks flying at up to 30 kilometres an hour, with— as time goes by—gusts to 100.

I know. I was once a goalie. Perhaps I should rephrase that: I was, and am, a goalie. I am just not a *practising* goalie. Being a goalie changes you, scars you, in many of the things you do. For being a goalie is a *way of life* that continues into adulthood. You react defensively when people ask you to do something. Comments like "Is there anything that can go wrong?" or "How can we protect ourselves on this one?" are not uncommon. One might even suggest that Canadians are a nation of goalies.

On the plus side, there is the uncanny ability to stand back and watch things unfold, like a spectator who is actually in the game. Given the nature of the position, the best goalers should be lawyers or hockey analysts. That is why when you look at what old goaltenders do when they retire— they are, yes, lawyers and analysts.

But I digress.

That winter started for me on a mild November night in the pine-panelled basement of Donald Ross, the best coach Montreal West minor hockey had ever seen. A hero of the Second World War, Mr. Ross lost his left leg in Normandy, and came back to Montreal to start a family of five children who including two girls who were champion swimmers. were all athletes. He was an executive in a company downtown and the police commissioner of our eight-man police force.

His son Dugie was my friend, a swimmer like his sisters and a tremendous hockey player. A wiry guy with a quick laugh and a quicker shot, he was always a threat from the blue line in. And his dad, Don Ross was going to be my coach that year. I was thrilled.

3

Don Ross was a great scout of hockey talent, as was clear to me as I looked around the room. The squad he had assembled was like a mini all-star team. There was big Timmy Manning, known for his fearsome end-to-end rushes, a mini Jean Béliveau. Tim must have been at least 5'6" - at 11 years old! There was Ross Galbraith—another big strong forward, and the guy who always seemed to be able to feed Dugie the right pass at the right time. Charles "Buster" Duff was Dugie's best buddy. Tim Trask had always been a solid defenceman in front of me at goal. Norman Campbell was smart and quick and was a team player with a huge smile. I wondered who all the other teams were left with to form their squads.

"Andy, would you like to see my wooden leg?"

This was a part of the ritual that took place for every new member of a Don Ross team. He would roll up the sleeve of his trousers and show us his prosthesis. We gasped as one. Then he calmly rolled down the trousers and said, "Okay boys, now that you have all seen the leg, let's talk a little hockey. You and I know the Reds will have great team this year. Now, let's just go down the roster. We start with Andy in goal. Now Andy, we are expecting you to carry a load for us. Are you keen?"

I was a bit apprehensive. "Sure, Mr. Ross, but I was thinking that I might like to play out this year a bit. Just to work on my skating, and to do something more interesting..." "But Andy, we drafted you as our goaltender (the way he said it made it sound so important). You know, it would be great to have you as our goalie. Let's just see how it works out."

So I was back in my place—between the pipes. Minding the store. Eating rubber. At ten-and-a-half years old my fate was sealed. I was a goalie. I didn't mind catching the pucks. And I didn't even mind the long stretches of watching the game. I didn't even mind being blamed if we lost a game. I really minded the cold.

Back in the winter of 1962-63 our town did not have an arena. The rink we played on was perched at the side of the escarpment that looks out over the Saint Lawrence River. For about four kilometres west across a bleak plain, there was nothing but railroad tracks, nothing to protect the rink from the winds that whipped across the river to the crest of the cliff and onto the rink. When the wind blew onto the rinks of Montreal West on a Saturday morning or any night, it was COLD.

In that kind of cold, the first things to go are the legs. The cold works into your body and takes over the skin one centimetre at a time. For the forwards and defencemen, their body heat keeps them oblivious to the cold.

Not the goalie. The cold paralysed me on that outdoor rink so quickly that I did not realize it. I would move back and forth, back and forth, until my body was accustomed to the lack of feeling below the waist. A few plays, a few stops and I was back struggling with the cold.

That is, until the end of the game. At game's end, we would all trudge into the chalet, a cement hut that housed all the hockey players on a Saturday morning. I would head down to the dark basement where our team dressed and undressed, and in the foul smell of cigarettes, coffee and sweat, someone—either the coach or my father—would unlash my pads and untie my skates, and the chilblains—the painful thawing of my feet—would begin. As the blood entered my frozen feet, I would cry and cry. And cry.

Normally a cold day meant ten minutes of crying. A little colder and there was screaming. A little warmer and it was just incredibly painful.

That I minded.

So going back into goal on those frozen days was not something to look forward to. However, the chance of winning the championship and earning bragging rights and a neat little championship crest for my windbreaker, seemed to compensate. So I agreed. I would be the goaltender for the Red Team. The team with all the best players.

Except Dane Baily.

Dane Baily was nothing short of phenomenal. He seemed to be able to score goals at will. If the media had been looking for the next Howe, Richard or Hull the way they seem to be searching for the Hockey Messiah today, someone would have done a feature on him. Dane would score six, seven, ten goals in a game. He made it look easy—he was a superb skater, close to the ice and able to turn on a dime—not a bad asset for an 11-year-old. He was smart, fast and an accurate shooter. With a wrist shot that allowed him to place a puck anywhere, anytime.

He made it look especially easy on me. His team, the Greys, beat us by scores of 5-1, 10-0, 7-2....the nightmares went on and on. And the other teams piled it on. But it was Dane Baily who was always in my nightmares. If I went down, he went high. If I covered the post he hit the far side. When I wanted to smother the puck, he plucked it out and got the rebound. If I watched him, he passed it to a teammate.

Our team did not take losing very well. And the reaction of all these great players was to rely exclusively on their individual effort. Unfortunately, hockey is a team game—something we seemed to forget the deeper the hole we were in. And the deeper the hole, the farther away my defencemen seemed to roam. Then the breakaways started.

There is nothing more terrifying than a player

approaching on a breakaway. From the far end of the rink, the opposing player approaches, gaining speed. The goaler checks the posts, sometimes rapping both with the butt end of his stick. The player shifts into higher gear as he crosses the blue line. The goaler inches out. The player makes a slight adjustment to approach at an angle, like an airplane approaching the runway.

The goalie adjusts and waits for the first move from the player. It is either a shot or a feint, called a deke. If a deke, the goalie has to wait for the shot, constantly telling himself "Wait!" and "Stand up!" For if he falls down, the next sight will be the puck flying over his prone body.

If the player waits and then shoots, by standing up the goalie gives up space (and opportunities) on the hard-to-reach sides of the goal—high on the stick side and low on the glove side. Whichever way I played a breakaway, I was never really able to master the technique.

Especially against Dane Baily.

By the time January rolled around, our team had lost every game. I was, frankly, fed up with being a losing goaler. So I decided on a special project. I would teach myself to skate and shoot better than I ever had.

I bought myself a light stick, which was easy to handle, a CCM "Comet." Compared to my goalie stick, it felt as if it was made of balsa wood. The only full-size outdoor rink was where we played a couple of kilometres away, and our family did not have a car. So each night I walked to the rink, carrying my stick and skates and wearing full equipment. This went on night after night. My parents thought I had lost my mind. But I had to do it.

I had a special routine. I would skate around the rink ten times. Then I would sprint around five times. Then starts and stops—the suicide drill. Blue line to red line, red line to blue line. Back and forth, back and forth. Then when I was exhausted from skating, I would go into the corner and shoot the puck against the boards, over and over again. Bang! Bang! The sound would echo around the rink.

Then I would imagine my own breakaway.

I would start in the corner to the left of the goal, skate to the middle of the ice close to the blue line and shoot the puck off the boards so that it bounced back to me just before centre ice. Then I would skate with longer strides, moving over the blue line to the right face-off circle. Just as I was over the line of the circle, I would bring my stick back behind me and let the puck fly. Time and again, I would see it go up and catch the left-hand mesh of the net.

High on the stick side.

Every time I would score. The fact there was no goalie, no defence and no forwards didn't matter.

After a couple of weeks of this secret practice, I was ready. Our schedule continued, with the defeats piling up and I was finding it quite disheartening. Finally, I got up the courage after practice to ask Mr. Ross if I could play "out" our final game. It was against the dreaded Grey team, featuring—who else—Dane Baily.

Reluctantly, he agreed. "I know what you have been through, Andy, and I sympathize. It is not easy being the goaler on a losing team. You have suffered enough. I will give you a shot. I'll ask Ross Galbraith to take over from you—he has been asking for a chance in goal."

I came home and told my parents that I was going to play forward, not goal, in our next game. Then my walking up the rink for the nightly practices made sense to them. My father took me aside and said that whatever happened, he was proud of me. Then he added in that slight Scottish lilt of his, "Fella, remember that sometimes, doing your best is just as good as winning." I paused to let it sink in. I thought it was a nice sentiment, but I would rather not lose!

So on a bright Saturday morning in late February, we left the chalet to play our final game. I felt strange, almost light, not wearing my goalie equipment. I skated across the ice to the wooden huts that acted as benches. And the game began.

It was clear to see that this was a "nothing" game for the Greys, who were going on to the playoffs while we were mired in the basement. For us it was important: we wanted to come close, to save our honour.

They scored early, but we tied it all at one with a goal from Dugie. They went ahead 2 to 1 on a goal by Dane and another, and they led us 3 to 1. Then their goalie was injured as the second period ended. When we came out for the third period, the Greys had a new man in goal: Dane Baily.

I could scarcely believe it. The player who had been my nemesis was in goal. If only I could get a shot on him!

The period began with Dugie's line (with Buster and Tim Manning) facing off. A few plays back and forth, but not much was happening, as Ross blocked everything that came his way and Dane was off in the goal at the other end.

Mr. Ross called out, "Okay, second line." and we hobbled out of the little wooden shelter onto the ice. The face-off was in our end, and I won it, but the puck was wrested away from me as I tried to take it up ice. The puck went to the point, a shot on goal from in front and—save—by Galbraith. He held on to the puck and the face-off was to his left.

I looked over to Norman Campbell on my left and down the ice beyond their defence. The puck dropped and was shot down the left side boards toward our goal. Norman stopped the puck behind me, then laid it up the left side at a slight angle, so the puck bounced off the boards and gently towards centre ice. As it hit the boards, I could see that it would go between the two defencemen and create a breakaway.

My breakaway.

I was already in pursuit. When I passed the blue line, it was within reach. Just after the red line, I corralled it. The defenceman behind me was just a memory. I was heading for the net.

I shifted to the right side to get a clear shot, crossed the blue line as I had practiced so many times before and looked up to see Dane coming out to cut the angle. I hit the top of the right hand face-off circle and drew my stick back as far as I could, then levered the puck with everything I had. My wrist flexed. And then I let it go.

There was no sound. The puck did not hit a blocker or a glove. There was no "thwack" off the stick or "boom" off the board. The puck hit the mesh, left hand, top shelf. High on the stick side. Very quietly.

I did not have to hear the crowd roar to know I

had scored. My teammates jumped on top of me in the corner of the rink. When I got up, I could see Dane's head just a little low, and I almost felt sorry for him. I went over to Norman and said "Great pass." He was beaming that huge smile of his.

I went back to the bench and Mr. Ross gave me a pat on the back and said "Good work, Andy." We did not score another goal and the game ended 3 to 2. It didn't matter. For us, to come that close was a win, and there was not one disappointed face after the game. Our season was over, but we could hold our heads high. We were laughing and joking as if we had just won the Stanley Cup.

As I watched the celebration, I thought of my father's words: "Sometimes, doing your best is just as good as winning."

The Playoff

By Andrew Caddell

If there was anything I wanted in life when I was 11 years old it was a Champion's crest. Made of a light cloth and red, blue, green or white, it was circular with a little athletic motif and a baseball bat or a hockey stick. It said, CHAMPIONS, the sport and the date. In my little world as a child, the little piece of cloth was the sign of someone who had "arrived."

In our little town of Montreal West, the crest or crests on the back of a windbreaker meant more than words. For the two thousand or so children in that little town, having one or more crests was equivalent to sporting immortality. One crest and you were a champ, two crests and you had potential. Three or more and you were a genuine athlete, in an era when that was pretty important, especially to an 11-year-old boy.

Some guys I knew had those crests covering their windbreakers. Instead of one or two crests on the chest of the jacket, they would be carefully placed in a geometric pattern on the back. Then they would grow out of their jackets and their moms would neglect to take off the crests, and pass them on to someone in the neighbourhood. So someone else—often it was a sibling—got to bathe in their reflective glory.

But for those who had something to prove, wearing as many crests as possible meant you preserved them. They were, after all, sacred. Besides, would you really WANT to have someone else wearing the symbols of your success? Never!

The Montreal Canadiens were the Stanley Cup champions five years in a row when I was young. They never loaned the Cup to anyone else or let anyone else call themselves "Stanley Cup Champions." Even their little brothers or sisters.

These older boys' jackets showed a sense of history: "PeeWee hockey 1959, CRA, one would say. Mosquito baseball, 1958, Bantam hockey, 1961."

I had a few baseball crests at that point in my life, but no hockey ones. I really wanted a hockey crest, but the year before our team had not won a single game. Not one! And I had been the goalie. And this year, pretty well the same players were coming out to play in our town league. Things looked pretty dismal.

Our coach, Mr. Ross, was optimistic, as a lot of us had grown over the previous year. And after a brief try at forward, I was ready to return to goal. It was not that I had resigned myself to it. I actually looked forward to playing goal. I had played a lot of ball hockey that summer and fall, and I felt ready to take up the challenge.

So were Tim Trask, Ross Galbraith, John Bernier, Charles "Buster" Duff and of course, Dugie Ross, the coach's son. I was hopeful they were ready to play as a real team. And we picked up some younger players who moved up. Mike Holding and Ross Owen. Mike was small and fast, and Ross was a cherubic but hard-plugging defenceman with a great shot.

The last year, I had faced about ten breakaways a game, when my teammates left me unprotected. This time, how would it be? I found out soon enough, when we won our first game in mid-December. It was a hard-fought battle, but amazingly, we won. It was the first time I had won a game since March of the year before. I was ecstatic.

The season continued that way. We were the number one team. We loved hockey that year. It became a really fun time, with parties after practices, and some truly spectacular games. We were the team to beat. And we won almost every game, slipped through the playoffs pretty easily, with scores galore and some near shutouts on my part.

So, we had made it to the final playoff game. It was March 2, an unheard-of late date for outdoor hockey. The ice would melt in the day and be flooded again at night, a good two–three inches of clear ice provided to us by that Master of the Hodgson Field ice rinks, Andy Smith.

There was one problem with the rink: the hot sun was being absorbed by the blue and red line markings. So, for this game, there would be only white paint where the lines would normally have been. It looked a little odd, but it was better than having our players drive though slush each time they hit the blue line.

The ice, aside from the odd lines, was perfect. The blue sky was mirrored off the sheen on the rink. It looked Forum-like. And given that Andy Smith Jr. was playing for us, I would not have expected anything less.

We arrived at the old Chalet at Hodgson Field at just after 9:00 a.m. that Saturday. A little early, but more than appropriate for the Championship game. I had hardly slept the night before.

Normally, both teams would have been dressing in the same space. Today was different. We dressed upstairs, while the Greys dressed in the space below. We were being segregated from each other, not because fights might break out, but simply because that is what you did when it was a Championship Game.

We laced up our skates and looked at each other with a certain pride that we had come this far, mixed with an apprehension that we might not get our crest. But we were determined to play our best game ever.

Mr. Ross came into the little room and began to speak. "Boys, we have come a long way this year. But we have not yet finished. I know that each of you is going to do his very best today. And if you do, we will win this championship. So, play well, play clean and skate as hard as you can. And Andy, just keep blocking those shots—your defencemen will do the rest."

He was a prophet. My defence was solid, and we got the scoring we needed from Dugie and Mike Holding. All in all, though, it was tight. The game was a back and forth affair, with goals traded between the teams. Skating was not easy as the ice was becoming progressively softer. I gave up a couple of goal-mouth scrambles, and at the end of regulation time, we were tied at two goals apiece. The first overtime period was surprisingly not that hard from my point of view. Both teams were wound up like tops, and really could not settle down. There were a lot of icings, no penalties and very few shots on goal. It was the calm before the storm.

We went into the second overtime period. The ice had become slushy. It was getting well past 11:00 and close to noon. No one knew when it would end. But the score remained 2-2.

Then it happened. The game broke open. The Greys took a face-off in our end. The puck slipped back to their left defenceman, and then he passed it over to the right side, to big Steven Meyer.

He hit it with all his strength, which was a lot, given he was 5 foot six and 130 pounds. It flew directly towards me, hard and low. It hit me in the pants, just off to the right of my jock, bounced down and hit the ice, rolling through my legs. The other team saw it and they were convinced they had scored. Cheers went up from beside the boards. Then sticks and gloves began to fly in the air.

But meanwhile, I had fallen backwards, out of instinct, to see if I could trap the rolling puck. I swatted behind me, my blocker hand on the goal line, and gingerly leaning down, bent my right knee to allow me to look. Sitting on the goal line, my blocker holding it still, was the puck. Only about one-quarter of it was over the line. For me, all was silence and in slow motion. The noise of the cheering was non-existent. All I could think of was "No goal."

I called to Dugie, who was standing right there. He shouted "No goal!!" and waved his arms. Then the referee, Ian Ross, Dugie's brother, came over and looked. He looked once, then again. He said "let me see this, Andy."

He stood in front of me, as I was still lying on the ice and waved his arms back and forth, calling out, "No goal."

There was silence. The other coach could not believe it. Nor could the players on either team. A cheer went up from our fans. Their players began to pick up their sticks and gloves. A more dejected group of boys you have rarely seen.

But the game was still deadlocked, in the second overtime period, and we were getting awfully close to noon. The ice was literally melting under our skates: the game was in serious jeopardy of being declared a draw.

After a few minutes, the teams lined up to my right for a face-off. The puck was dropped, and they shot toward the net. I turned it aside, and Buster Duff passed it up to Johnny Bernier. He took off like a rocket. He deked one way, and then another. He went into the corner, still with the puck, passed it out to Buster Duff, and back to his stick. IN the net!!

Then it was our turn to go berserk. Sticks flew everywhere, gloves, you name it. Then we lined up to shake hands in the soggy, watery rink, as the sun beat down on us. When I came to Steven Meyer, he just glowered at me, and then smiled.

"Nice game.... nice...*save.*" Some of their players on the other team said quietly, "it was in."

Within a day or two, life went on, we got our crests, and our moms sewed them on to our windbreakers in time for the baseball season to begin.

As the years went by and we began to attend the same high school, I became friends with Steven Meyer, who had changed his name to Johnson when his mom re-married. After high school, we worked summers out west together, we hiked and climbed, we exchanged Christmas cards when he moved to the States. But whatever the distances and the time, we stayed in touch.

Every few years, I would get together with Steven for a drink or a meal. And inevitably, the subject of that championship game would come up. And then the controversy would explode again.

"How could you not win? Your captain, the referee and your coach were all from the same family!"

"Ah Steve, you are such a sore loser! That goal never went in!"

"That is what you say! I shot that puck so hard, it had to go in."

"It didn't make it all the way...."

"That's what you say! "

And the conversation would go on and on, with a bit of teasing from both sides, and a lot of laughs. There we were—10, 20, 30, and now 50-odd years later—arguing about a little hockey game of 11-year-olds on a Saturday morning in March.

Long after my beloved crests had disintegrated from my well-worn windbreaker, long after the windbreaker had been passed on from one neighbourhood kid to another, our friendship endured. And that was what really mattered.

The Game

by Dave Stubbs

At twenty-five minutes past two this morning, a bushy-haired blonde veteran of hockey, Hector Kilrea, a sturdy, scarlet-clad form wearing the white emblem of Detroit Red Wings, went pounding tirelessly down the battle-scarred, deep-cut Forum ice, trying to pilot a puck that was bobbling crazily over the rough trail, almost out of control.

It looked like another of the endless unfinished plays—when suddenly, in shot the slim form of a player, who through this long, weary tide of battle that ebbed and flowed had been almost unnoticed. He swung his stick at the bobbling puck, the little black disc straightened away, shot over the foot of Lorne Chabot, bit deeply into the twine of the Montreal Maroon cage. And so Modere Bruneteau, clerk in a Winnipeg grain office, leaped to fame as the player who ended the longest game on professional hockey record.

- Elmer Ferguson
Montreal Herald, Wednesday, March 25, 1936

They played a National Hockey League double-header eight weeks ago, and the Dallas Stars eliminated the Edmonton Oilers in their Western Conference quarter-final after 57 minutes and 34 seconds of overtime. A long, grueling night of playoff hockey, to be sure, yet only a pale pretender to the throne.

As this season lumbers along to its summer-time end, Phil Caddell might even suggest that Joe Nieuwendyk, who scored the winner for Dallas, couldn't have tied the skate-laces of

Detroit's Modere (Mud) Bruneteau, a hockey hero for the ages.

At the Forum on March 24 and into the wee hours of March 25, 1936, the Detroit Red Wings and Montreal Maroons played a triple-header, nearly three full games, in the first match of their best-of-five semi-final playoff series.

Sixty-three years ago, Phil Caddell was still on his north-end bench seat at 2:25 a.m.—flat out and sound asleep, he admits—when Mud Bruneteau scored the game's only goal, lashing the Red Wings' 67th shot past Maroons goaler Lorne Chabot at 16:30 of the sixth overtime period. The teams had played 116 minutes, 30 seconds of extra time, 176:30 including 60 minutes of regulation, to decide the longest game in NHL history.

In the other crease, Detroit's Normie Smith was numb, unbeaten by 90 Maroon shots. He hadn't lost 12 pounds through perspiration, he merely had transferred the weight to his saturated peak-cap, long-johns and leather goal pads that were stuffed with soggy horsehair.

"You know, we figured it was going to go on all night," says Caddell, who will turn 86 in a few weeks. "And our pact was, we weren't leaving until it was over. Whether we were awake or not."

- There was quite an array of clerics in boxes on the east side, among whom was Ven. Archdeacon Gower-Rees and the Very Rev. Dean Carlisle. They stayed through 100 minutes of overtime, and then called it a day, or rather a night. But they weren't alone. Many others toiling on bankers' hours had gone long ago.
-Baz O'Meara, Montreal Star

Until that night, the longest game on record had been played on April 3, 1933 in Toronto, going 104 minutes and 46 seconds into overtime. The Maple Leafs' Ken (Cagey) Doraty finally scored to defeat Boston 1-0.

The NHL was an eight-team league in 1935-36, four clubs in both the Canadian and American divisions. The Canadiens, who late in the season had traded Lorne Chabot to the Maroons for three players, including a rookie winger named

Toe Blake, were on the outside looking in as the playoffs began. They had finished in the Canadian cellar with 11 victories in 48 games.

The Maroons were the defending Stanley Cup champions, and in the opinion of Montreal's English newspapers—The Gazette, the Star, and the best sports page in town, the Herald—they were a cinch to repeat. Their first post-season test would be the Red Wings, champions of the American Division.

The series opened at the Forum at 8:30 p.m. on Tuesday, March 24, before a crowd estimated at 9,000, a thousand less than capacity. With two friends, Val Traversy and Herbie Howe, Phil Caddell walked to the arena from National Breweries, where he worked as a junior clerk earning $40 a month.

"There were tickets galore. We just walked up and bought 'em at a window on the sidewalk, and I'd be surprised if we spent more than 50 cents for our (unreserved) rush-end seats," says Caddell, who was 22.

"We just went to see three periods of hockey. How could we possibly know we'd get nine?"

- The boys were so tired they were skating from memory and shooting by ear. The referees were so weary they could only blow feeble toots on their tin whistles. Here's to Hec Kilrea, who started the play that sent the fans home for breakfast!

- Philip Morris Navy Cut cigarette ad, The Star

Phil (Pip) Caddell was born in Brantford, Ont., on July 7, 1913 and moved to Lachine as an infant when his father went off to war. One of four children, he was seven when his family moved to Edinburgh, where he worshipped Scottish Olympic track star Eric Liddell, the central character of the film Chariots of Fire.

He was 14 when they returned to Lachine, and as a young caddie at a local golf course he often stood pop-eyed at the first tee, ogling hockey's fabulous Cleghorn brothers, Odie and Sprague, and two living legends: Howie Morenz and Aurel Joliat.

"That's the difference between hockey then and now," Caddell says. "The players then lived in your neighbourhood year-round. You grew up around them, and they were part of you. Either you knew them, or you knew someone who knew them."

Before long he was going to McGill to watch college football, or riding the streetcar from his home to the Forum, where he'd queue to buy a ticket—always in the rush-end of the rink—to watch his beloved Maroons. He didn't play a lot of hockey himself. "There was only one rink in upper Lachine," he recalls, "and very seldom did it have decent ice."

- Nearly three tons of snow was swept from the ice between periods. The surface remained hard, but eventually the puck refused to lie down and be good. Bert Newbury, Forum superintendent, made suggestions to Frank Calder, president of the NHL, that a little longer period of rest be given so that the ice might be flooded, but he stoutly refused all such offers of advice. Ten

minutes rest was all the boys needed, according to the president.

-Al Parsley, The Herald

No one had expected the Maroons to win the Stanley Cup a year earlier, least of all the publicity director of National Breweries, the corporate parent of a number of ale and lager brands. One of its labels, Black Horse, was enormously popular as much for its stables as its beer; the brewery owned a number of mighty Percherons it would loan to rural Quebec horsemen for breeding.

Reginald Joseph (Hooley) Smith, the Maroons captain, coveted the valuable horses and apparently convinced the brewery to give him one should his club win the 1934-35 Cup. Ranked fourth in the regular season, the Maroons knocked off Chicago, New York and finally upset top-ranked Toronto in three straight games to win the title.

A young brewery office boy named Phil Caddell, in his first year on the job, was immediately dispatched to every beauty parlour on Ste. Catherine St. to buy all the black hair dye he could find. Caddell never knew for certain, but he assumed that the publicity director, perhaps in deep with his bosses for an offer he couldn't deliver, was planning to give Hooley Smith a brown nag painted black. But in The Gazette's archives is a tiny news brief published in April, 1935, covering a ceremony attended by 2,000 fans at which Smith indeed was presented with the genuine article.

Detroit goaler Smith played like a stallion. The highest total of shots that bounced off his sprightly, alert frame in a period was in the third, when he turned aside 15 smashing drives. In the third period of overtime, again in the fourth, as Maroons time and again rallied their forces to crash his citadel, he stopped 13 in each.

-Ferguson, The Herald

Normie Smith broke into the NHL with the Maroons in 1931, playing 20 games before he was accidentally crushed by then-teammate Howie Morenz in a goalmouth scramble and sidelined for the season. He languished in the minors for two years and took to wearing a peaked cap, which he found cut the glare from the overhead lights. In 1934, he was signed by Detroit manager and coach Jack Adams.

Not only did Smith shut out the Maroons over nearly nine periods of this incredible game, he blanked them again in Game 2 and wasn't beaten until 12:02 of the first period of Game 3, giving him a shutout streak of 248:32, which remains an NHL record. The Wings swept the Maroons and then beat Toronto in the final to win their first of two consecutive Stanley Cups.

Smith's 90 saves in one game (92, according to some reports) are listed in the Guinness Book of World Records.

"We could not believe they kept coming out to play, and as Maroon fans we could not believe the stops the Detroit boy kept making," says Caddell, sitting in an easy chair, chewing on a peppermint and warming to the memories.

Caddell's war medals, and those of an uncle, are framed above his bed in the Lachine seniors home where he lives. He was widowed four years ago, and on a table at his bedside is a framed photograph of Elga Ramsey—Duckie, he called her—whom he married on March 23, 1945, two days after returning from battle. He has four children—Susan, Ian, Andrew and Graham—and 11 grandchildren. Most of them love hockey, and all of them adore the tale about Hooley Smith, the nag and the black hair dye.

- Bucko McDonald, rugged steak-destroyer, almost wrecked the Maroon forward line with his crashing bodychecks. He flattened everyone but Chabot.

- Ferguson, The Herald

Wilfred Kennedy (Bucko) McDonald, a beefsteak-and-potatoes man of 205 pounds, earned his pay and more on this night. Renowned for his physical style, a Red Wings fan offered him $5 for every Maroon he leveled. Nine periods and 37 punishing bodychecks later, the fan happily forked over $185, enough to buy Bucko a few prime sirloins.

The Maroons' Joe Lamb didn't see action until the "second" game. He later told reporters,

"After this, I'm going to have my steak at around 8 o'clock instead of 3 in the afternoon!"

At least a few fans chose shut-eye over sustenance. Published reports vary on how many spectators were left at the end, but Caddell, who finally was awakened by the cheers—"It was more a sigh of relief," one columnist wrote—recalls having enough room to stretch out on his rushend bench.

The girls working the refreshment booths on the promenade deck, who usually would close up shop by 10 p.m., were still serving cakes and coffee four hours later.

During intermissions, players were sipping tea and coffee laced with brandy, then lying on their backs with their legs up on benches to improve circulation. The two referees, Ag Smith and Bill Stewart (the latter the grandfather of current NHL official Paul Stewart), stopped taking their skates off, afraid they wouldn't be able to lace up their boots over surely swollen feet.

Finally, at 2:25 a.m., a 21-year-old rookie from St. Boniface, Man., played the hero. The following morning, Maroons goaler Lorne Chabot presented right-winger Mud Bruneteau with the puck that ended the game.

"Gee whiz, gee whiz, that's swell," an overwhelmed Mud told reporters as he twirled the prize in his hands.

Only a few hours earlier, the last streetcar to Lachine having long since departed, Phil Caddell had hiked up to Val Traversy's house in Westmount to nap on a parlour couch. He was back at work at 8:30 a.m.

- Bruneteau scored just about the time the milkman was starting to steam out on his morning rounds. The fans had steeled themselves for a fluke goal long before the tally came. The one that broke the contest was luck-tinged, but fans did not cavil at it. It came as a welcome relief.

- O'Meara, The Star

Mud Bruneteau, a Winnipeg grain-commissions clerk for Montreal-born Red Wings owner James

Norris, died April 15, 1982. He is exclusively celebrated for the historic overtime goal he scored in his first-ever playoff game, which while understandable is also a disservice to his contribution to hockey.

Bruneteau played 11 seasons for Detroit, scoring 162 goals in 488 games. He went down to the Red Wings' farm club in Omaha in 1946-47 and retired to coach the Knights in 1948-49, handpicked by Jack Adams to nurture the next generation of Wings. That season he became the first professional coach of Terry Sawchuk, one of the greatest goalies of all time.

A gifted, patient communicator, Bruneteau taught the young Sawchuk the finer points of the position, and Sawchuk, a future Hall of Famer, frequently credited his coach for his development. Mud Bruneteau scored once more in the playoff season of 1935-36, and his name is engraved on the Stanley Cup three times.

But when the Red Wings and Montreal Maroons met for Game 2 that March 26, a tidy, quick 3-0 Detroit victory, there was at least one fan not on the Forum's rush-end benches.

"Most probably," Phil Caddell says, "I simply couldn't afford the ticket."

The Black Horse

by Philip Caddell

It all began as an innocent conversation between two men late one night: one man was an athlete and the other was a businessman. It ended up with a photo in the paper, and me with black dye all over my hands.

It is a true story, though, I assure you.

Back in 1935, I was working at the Dawes brewery in Montreal, where I was a clerk. I was pleased to be a clerk, as that was one step above being an office boy, which is how I joined Dawes, or as we all called it, "The Brewery."

We were in the midst of the Great Depression, a period when the economy was pretty bad, and even people who had been wealthy before the Depression were struggling. The Great Depression hit in about 1931, the year I graduated from high school in Lachine, a town west of Montreal.

It was like that across the country, and across the world. My family was poor, but we were lucky: we never went on "the dole," although both my brothers worked, and my brother Charlie did "ride the rails" of the trains out west in search of work. My mother was a very proud woman and she depended on me and my two brothers to support her and my teen-aged sister. The five of us were crowded into a little house our cousin "Minnie" Dawes owned. It was so small, we called it "the Bonnet Box," as it looked like a little hatbox.

I was happy to have a job, as not many people those days did. It was also thanks to my cousin Minnie that I had the job, as her husband owned the brewery.

Meanwhile the President of the company was my cousin Minnie's nephew, Norman Dawes, so he was sort of a relative. His brother, Kenneth, was the Vice President, and he was quite the sports fan. It made for a good combination, as he did a lot of the brewery's public relations, but quite frankly, he was not the sharpest pencil in the box. He had a reputation for doing nasty practical jokes and he sometimes said or did things he learned to regret.

Just the same, he loved hockey, and so did I, and so I could not help but envy his ability to go to all the best professional sports events. Especially the Montreal Maroons games at the Montreal Forum. He had great tickets to those games. I, on the other hand, had to settle for the cheapest seats in the house: the general admission tickets for 25 cents that gave access to the long benches at the far end of the main entrance. To get the best location, my friends and I had to run to the other end when the doors opened. So everyone called it "The Rush End."

There were two professional hockey teams in Montreal at that time, the other team was the Montreal Canadiens, which everyone knows as the greatest NHL team ever. They shared the Montreal Forum, and they were fierce rivals with the Maroons: fights often broke out in the stands and even between newspaper reporters covering the teams.

But in the 1930s, the Canadiens were struggling at the gate and on the ice. They had some good years, but now they were in danger of missing the playoffs, and the bad economy did not help a bit. The Maroons on the other hand, were a bit more competitive, and had many top rank players. The Maroons were my team, and the team Kenneth Dawes and everyone in Lachine supported.

So, Kenneth had great seats, and he got to hobnob with all the players. Because after a hockey game, the players would have a free Black Horse Ale with him.

One night, after a game, he was having a drink with the captain of the Team, Reginald "Hooley"

Smith, who began to talk to him about the quite remote chance of the Maroons winning the Stanley Cup.

The Toronto Maple Leafs were the powerhouse of the time. They had the famed "Kid Line" of Harvey "Busher" Jackson, Charlie Conacher and Joe Primeau. They were an all-star team all on their own. The Maroons were in fourth place at that point in the season, and not many people gave them any chance of winning the Cup.

Even the most dedicated fans like me, or like Kenneth Dawes.

Of course, as long as they made the playoffs, they had as good a chance as anyone else to win the Cup, except that they had not set the league on fire in the 48 games they had played that year. So, although Kenneth was a very passionate supporter of the Maroons, as we all were, his heart did not overrule his head.

But "Hooley" Smith would not let up. He was convinced they were going to win the Cup. And when "Hooley" got something in his head, there was little that could stop him: he was like a runaway train going downhill. He had come to the Maroons from the Ottawa Senators in a trade in 1927, after being suspended for one whole month after he beat another fellow senseless in the Cup finals the previous season.

Along with Nels Stewart and Babe Siebert, he became part of the dreaded "S" line, which terrorized opponents for years. At 5'10" and 180 pounds, he was a giant in those days, when players were a lot smaller. And he used his size to his advantage. He also had the annoying habit of chewing tobacco in a game and spitting tobacco juice at the goalies before he shot the puck at them.

So "Hooley" was not a character to meddle with. And yet Kenneth Dawes and "Hooley" were getting into a pretty intense discussion about the Maroons' chances. It might have been the beer they were drinking, or it might have been a bit of male bravado but evidently, the conservation went something like this:

"Mr. Dawes, I am convinced we are going to win the Stanley Cup."

"Well, Mr. Smith, I respect your ability but I cannot say that I agree with you."

"Well, let us place a little wager on this," said "Hooley" Smith.

"What do you propose?" responded Kenneth Dawes.

"Well, I have a little farm, and I could really use one of those beautiful black Percheron horses you have to pull your beer wagons. You know the ones – the symbols of Black Horse Ale."

Kenneth Dawes was astonished. The Black Percheron Horses were known everywhere in Quebec as being the most valuable workhorses that existed. The Dawes family had a huge pasture near us in Lachine where the horses were bred and fed. The family took a great deal of pride in the black Percherons: they imported them into Canada years before, and had improved the breed over time.

The black horses were enormous, standing 16 hands (about eight feet) high, and weighing up to 1800 pounds. They could pull a huge plough on their own. It was only when mechanized tractors became popular that the Percherons fell into disuse. And the Dawes Brewery made a fortune by loaning them out to breed to farmers who could afford it. And the most popular beer in Quebec at that time was Dawes Black Horse Ale, with a picture of a Percheron Horse on the label. The black horse was everywhere—on advertising, playing cards, pen knives, pencil sharpeners, bottle openers and calendars.

"But those horses are worth a fortune." Kenneth Dawes replied.

"Then you don't want to wager?" needled "Hooley" Smith as the players gathered round. "Fine," said Kenneth Dawes, "If you win the Stanley Cup, you will get a Percheron. But what will you pay if you lose this bet?"

"Don't worry Mr. Dawes, I am NOT going to lose. The Maroons are going to the Cup."

Now I loved the Maroons as much as anyone else did. When I immigrated to Canada from Scotland the closest thing to my favourite sport, rugby, was hockey. I could not skate worth a darn, but I loved to watch it. The checking, the speed, the skill, was all so spectacular. And it was a great time to take a few friends and run down to the benches at the Rush End of the Forum.

The Maroons were my team, but I never thought they would come close that year. The Leafs and the New York Rangers were pretty strong. And in the middle of the season, nothing was happening. The Maroons were not getting the production they needed from their better lines and players like "Hooley" Smith were stuck in major slumps.

So, taking a bet in mid-season that the Maroons would win the Cup was not that difficult, because the way they were going, they would be eliminated pretty quick. They would have to improve in the last half of the season to make a run at it.

As luck would have it, they did. And that is when things became complicated.

The Maroons went on a winning streak that surprised even the most ardent fans. The best players began to click: "Hooley" Smith, Lionel "Big Train" Conacher, "Babe" Siebert and a rookie named Hector "Toe" Blake started potting goals. In the nets, Alex Connell was spectacular.

As the 48-game schedule wound down, the Maroons were in second place in the "Canadian" division, behind the powerhouse Leafs. Their rivals, the Canadiens, came third, nine points behind. The Leafs had scored 157 goals, the Maroons only 123. Then the playoffs began. The Canadiens were eliminated quickly by the New York Rangers, while the Maroons won a tight series, scoring only one goal in a total goals series, but shutting out the Chicago Blackhawks.

The Maroons then took on the Rangers and dispatched them. So now they were facing the Leafs, our hated rivals, in the final for the Stanley Cup. Who would have known it would come this far? "Hooley" Smith, perhaps. Although the Toronto lads were almost as disliked as the cross-town rivals, the Canadiens, I think Kenneth Dawes might have been privately cheering for them. After all, he could lose a horse if the Maroons won.

But win they did, in a four-game final that brought them their first Stanley Cup. Fans in Montreal were jubilant. It was the greatest thing for the fans of the Maroons, like me. And it was especially satisfying to the players, like "Hooley" Smith.

As soon as the Maroons scored their last goal of the last game, it was obvious that Kenneth Dawes would have to pay up. There was only one problem: when he looked into the company's rules, it turned out that even though he was Vice President of the company and his name was Dawes, he did not own the Percheron horses—the company's shareholders did. He was an important shareholder and so were his relatives like my mother's cousin Minnie, but others were individual investors on the stock market. And in the Great Depression, investors were pretty scarce.

You should also understand that the Percheron horses were very valuable, and farmers paid a lot to have their horses bred to them. The brewery considered them very important assets for the company. So, giving them away to hockey players, even star hockey players who had won the Stanley Cup, was just not done. And yet, the Maroons were the toast of the town. Turning down "Hooley" Smith was not going to be good for the image of the most popular brewery in Quebec!

Kenneth Dawes was in a tight spot. Now, I do not know whose idea it was, whether it was Norman's or one of his bright boys in charge of operations, but someone suggested that he give the hockey player a horse—it just did not have to be a "Black Horse." It could be black, but it did not have to be a fresh young Percheron.

And that is where I got involved.

"Caddell!" my boss called to me one morning. "We have a special assignment for you."

"What is that, sir?"

"Here is thirty dollars."

Now, thirty dollars was more than I made in two weeks! I couldn't imagine what on earth they wanted me to do with that much money. He soon told me.

"Go out on Saint Catherine Street to every beauty shop there is—and buy every single container, bottle or tin of black hair dye you can get your hands on."

"And then?" I asked.

"And then make your way back to the stables in back of the brewhouse. Be there at five this evening."

I did as I was told, and came back laden down with black hair dye. From every single beauty parlour in downtown Montreal.

At 5:00 sharp, my co-worker Val Traversy and I reported to the stables behind the brewhouse, and made our way to a large room off the stables. And standing there was one of the biggest old horses I had ever seen. Almost as big as the big Black Percherons that pulled the beer wagons.

But it was an old Percheron, long past retirement age. A bit sway-backed and tired, but still a Percheron. But a grey horse, not a black one. Because when Percherons get old, they turn grey. So this Percheron was not black. And it was our job to remedy that.

Suddenly the thirty dollars, the black hair dye and the horse in front of me came together. My friend Val and I were to deal with Kenneth Dawes's problem: we were going to paint a horse.

Black.

We set to work, and after an all-night session painting that huge horse, there stood the biggest, blackest, dark as night, worn down Percheron horse you could ever imagine. Soon it was dry, and we were ready to unveil it. We took it back to the stables, and the next morning my boss came in, pleased as punch.

"Caddell, great work! Here is twenty dollars more for you and your friend. Now don't tell anyone about this!"

So I didn't. Not when they took the horse out of the stable and combed him down, and not when they took him to a fancy ceremony where Kenneth Dawes presented the big black horse to Reginald Joseph "Hooley" Smith. And not even when the picture of "Hooley" and the horse and Kenneth Dawes appeared in the newspaper, with thousands of people present.

But I couldn't help telling people a few years later. And whenever I told anyone, we would imagine what "Hooley" Smith must have been thinking when somewhere on some farm, somewhere in Canada, sometime in the summer of 1935, when the first heavy rain came and washed away all the black hair dye from that big grey horse!

The Coin

By Dave Stubbs

There aren't any signs at the city limits of Kindersley, Sask., to announce that you're entering the hometown of Dick Meissner.

Nor will you find a Meissner Drive on any street map of Prince Albert, Sask., the hockey hotbed of the northern prairies where Dick learned to play the game.

Don't look for an arena named in his honour, or any trace of him among the skyscrapers of downtown Toronto, among the NHL legends whose careers are remembered in the Hockey Hall of Fame. But until recently you would have found Dick Meissner in a desk drawer in my office.

Well, kind of.

Since 1962, Dick, or a tiny piece of him, has followed me everywhere, looking up off a yellow plastic coin that spilled from a box of jelly-powder dessert mix into my hands when I was 6 years old. For some reason, the coin is the last real piece of childhood sports memorabilia I've saved. But as I thought about this little disc not long ago, rolling it in my hand, I picked up the telephone and found something better.

I found Dick Meissner himself, a rugged right-winger who played 171 games for the Boston Bruins and New York Rangers from 1959-65. This story is how I finally came to talk to the man who had travelled with me for most of my life, without his ever knowing it.

I collected hockey cards as a boy, chewing probably hundreds of little sticks of stale pink bubblegum that came in the packages.

My friends and I didn't treasure them as boys and girls do today, who put their cards in plastic sleeves, then store them in binders. We'd shuffle them, toss them up against walls, trade them and, with a clothespin, attach them to the frames of our bicycles and stick them into the spokes, where they'd make a great racket (we thought they made our bikes sound like motorcycles) until they'd finally disintegrate.

I also collected Bee Hive pictures, which were very popular from the 1930s through the late 1960s, when Ontario's St. Lawrence Starch Company stopped making them.

There was a paper collar on the top of every can of Bee Hive corn syrup, a sticky-sweet treat you'd spread on your toast or pour on your ice cream. Your mom would buy Bee Hive every week, whether she needed it in her cupboard or not, and you'd mail in that paper collar in exchange for a black and white photo of your favourite NHL hockey player. I was never happier to see the mailman than the day he pulled a brown envelope, addressed to me, out of his satchel.

I had dozens of Bee Hive pictures, mostly the Montreal Canadiens; some collectors today have many hundreds, and they're worth a lot of money.

I also had a few plastic coins, which were available in small boxes of jelly powder and available in a few other food products as well.

This is where I found Dick Meissner one day, the same gentleman I still have so many years later.

To describe Dick Meissner's career as unremarkable is not to be critical, because the NHL before expansion—that is to say, the six-team league before 1967—was built on the strong backs of many players like him. For every super-star like Gordie Howe, Jean Béliveau, Bobby Hull or Frank Mahovlich, there were dozens of average guys like Dick Meissner skating in the shadows, working hard to earn a living.

Dick scored 11 NHL goals, assisted on 15 more and spent 37 minutes in the penalty box, the highlight of 14 years in professional hockey that took him from Rhode Island to Seattle and nearly a dozen other minor-pro cities.

Dick was an 18-year-old junior with the Flin-Flon Bombers when he signed a $7,500 Bruins contract for the 1959-60 season.

"I have a lot of good memories of the NHL," he told me. "At the time, it was a very, very difficult league to play in because there weren't many positions available."

In fact, there were only 120 jobs in the NHL in Dick's day. In today's 30-team NHL, there are about 600. All these years later, Dick can close his eyes and still see himself as a rookie scoring his first big-league goal.

"It was against the New York Rangers at Madison Square Garden against Gump Worsley, in my fourth game," he said, as though it was only yesterday.

But even at 5-foot-11 and 228 pounds, Dick hadn't the strength to lift the Bruins, who were quite terrible, and he never knew what it was like to skate in the playoffs.

The history books best remember Boston's 1961-62 season for a 20-game losing streak, only 15 wins in a 70-game schedule. The Bruins had the NHL's weakest offence and by far its most awful defence.

And yet, history also remembers that year for the signing of 14-year-old Bobby Orr, who would become perhaps the NHL's best-ever defenceman, to a developmental contract.

Dick's knees were almost as bad as Bobby's. Five times he had knee surgery, which left him limping through much of his career.

He wound up with New York for 35 games in 1963-64 and one more contest in '64-65, his last in the NHL. In fact, a broken wrist suffered with the Rangers proved far more painful years down the road—Dick fell a single game short of qualifying for his league pension, a nice monthly paycheque from the league.

Not that he regrets a minute of his playing days. During his final minor-pro season in 1971, Dick moved to Portland, Ore., where he went to work as a general contractor. He has three grown children who know little of his NHL career, though he's collected a good bit of memorabilia for them to learn.

Dick especially cherishes a brick he was sent from old Boston Garden, his home arena, when it was knocked down to make room for a modern new rink. The game remains an important part of his life: his younger brother, Barrie, played six games with the Minnesota North Stars in the late 1960s. His nephew, Landon Wilson, has played in the NHL since 1995, for four different teams.

"I watch hockey today on television, but I do miss the days of the original six league," Dick admitted. "You'll just never get those great rivalries again. And tough? John Ferguson, Orland Kurten-bach, Léo Boivin, Fernie Flaman, Lou Fontinato—they don't make 'em any tougher than those boys."

From 1960-69, you'd find those heavyweights, and every other NHL player, on silver-dollar-sized coins in boxes of Salada tea, Shirriff dessert powders and potato-chip bags.

You could trade a complete, mint-condition six-team set for many thousands of dollars today, although my 1961-62 Dick Meissner is worth very little, having been badly scratched over the years.

But I'd never sell my coin of Dick, because I never considered it an investment. In fact, I scarcely considered him at all, no matter that how little attention I paid him he never strayed on the road from my childhood. For many years he has remained only a face on a plastic coin. Until now.

At the end of our delightful conversation, I told him I'd like to send him my Sherriff coin, a souvenir for his children perhaps, or at least a token of thanks for sharing his memories of his days in the NHL.

"No, thank you," Dick told me. "I already have one, believe it or not. But give me your address. I've got a few photos of some of the old guys I'd like to send you."

My new and old friend Dick Meissner did just that, and today I have many great pictures of him in his Boston Bruins sweater.

My little plastic coin is still in my office. But I've taken it out of my desk drawer, and now it's in a place of honour on a bookcase, where I look at it and smile each and every day.

The Gentleman

By Andrew Caddell

My Great-Aunt Elga was a sweet and gentle spinster who would not hurt a soul. And in a life spanning almost nine decades, she never did. But she loved the game of hockey, a sport that is rough and tumble and clearly not for the faint of heart. Even though she never played it, it was in her blood. And that is how she fell in love with Jean Béliveau.

Growing up in Quebec City as the last child in a family of eleven, she had four big, strong, athletic brothers and four sisters who were no slouches when it came to sports. Their mother, Emily Andrews LeMesurier, named each of her children with a moniker that reflected her penchant for the unorthodox: in an era that made a virtue of being the same, she gave them names that would stand out: Garnet, Claude, Percy, Sidney, Pearl, Irene, Olla and Estelle.

Elga's own unusual name came from a local newspaper story. In the fall of 1894, a ship docked in Quebec City with passengers immigrating to Canada. A photographer caught sight of an attractive young girl, probably from Eastern Europe, whose name was Elga. My great-grandmother Emily saw the photo on the front page of the local newspaper and gave the name to her daughter, who was born a few days later.

Elga was a bit shy and something of the runt of the family—photos from the time show a lovely little girl with long brown hair, big eyes and a sweet face. She went off to teacher's college in

Montreal in 1912. Two years later, her older brother Garnet and many of her friends went off to war. It was the last time she would see them.

The summer of 1914 had been one of parties and gaiety, the joys of still being young and full of energy. And it was a hot summer: the sun shone almost every day. The LeMesurier family undertook their annual ritual to escape the heat of Quebec City and take the train to Kamouraska, the small village about 100 miles downriver where they spent the summer. It was a summer in the Lower St. Lawrence without a care in the world. There was tennis on their tennis court, golf just adjacent in their big field stretching out to the St. Lawrence River, taffy pulls (where taffy would be twisted on a stick from a huge hot pot) for a hundred, and great fun with their friends day and night.

The assassination of Austria's Archduke Ferdinand in June of 1914 was not big news. It was buried in the back pages of the newspapers that arrived with the evening mail train from Quebec City. The crowds of young men standing outside the Kamouraska post office in the after-dinner evening light would have taken the post and newspapers home and not given a second thought to the impending conflict.

The summer flew by, and the LeMesurier house on the hill hummed. Summer romances abounded. It was, by all accounts, an idyllic life for these young people, born just before the turn of the new century.

Then the summer was over, and their innocence and youth with it.

The Great War began swiftly, and, believing it would last only a few months or, at most, a year, the young men of Quebec City enlisted in droves to save the Empire they had just arrived from, or to rescue the mother country, France. From the main base in Valcartier outside of the city, they trooped up and down the Grand Allée and paraded along the Plaines d'Abraham in their newly-made uniforms.

My aunt and her friends came out to see all the handsome soldiers. No one could imagine the horrors of the Somme and Verdun or the mustard gas of Ypres. It was unthinkable that 60,000 Canadians would die in battle in the next four years.

It was mustard gas that would take the life of Elga's brother Garnet less than a year later, in a vicious attack on Ypres. His body was never found and lies beneath the poppies in Flanders Fields.

For Aunt Elga and her friends, the absence of men during the war became a part of their lives. But then it ended and she and her friends were by and large, still alone. When asked years later why she never married, she said, "the boys went away, and they never came back."

After graduation from teacher's college in Montreal a few years after the war, Elga became a schoolteacher, and taught thousands of children in Quebec from 1920 to 1955. In the summer, she and her sister Pearl would take their mother downriver to Kamouraska from the last day of school to Labour Day. In the winter, Elga would teach her classes, and spend free time skating, cross-country skiing, and walking along the

Terrasse Dufferin in front of the Chateau Frontenac. When her mother died at 96 in late 1947, the ritual continued.

Then in 1949, a young man came to Quebec City to play for the local hockey team. His name was Jean Béliveau.

Jean Béliveau had played hockey for Victoriaville, and was the player of an era. Big and strong, he had the smooth moves, stickhandling grace and skating prowess that made him stand out like no other young player in all of the province of Quebec at the time. He said he learned all those moves by playing shinny with 30 kids in the old outdoor rinks in his home town, as "it was the only way you could hang on to the puck."

He had such talent, size and presence that in old photos of his school hockey team, he stands out among the rest. There was no question that he was destined for greatness. But he had more than that. His movie-star looks, charm and intelligence won him many admirers off the ice as well as on. At six foot four inches (1 m 92), he was a giant in a small man's sport, but just as quick and very powerful. A popular song of the time, talking about a big and powerful man suited Béliveau, and from that moment on, he was known as "Le Gros Bill."

In 1949, he began playing for the Quebec Citadelles Junior team and started making a name for himself. Then in 1950, he moved up to the amateur Quebec Aces team in the Quebec Senior League, and the team became legendary in those parts. The centre of the legend was Jean himself. As his popularity grew, there was not enough space to hold all the fans like my Aunt Elga, who came to see him, so they built a bigger arena: Le Colisée became known as "the House that Jean built."

He was so famous that he was said to be receiving a salary of $20,000 a year and on top of that, he did not have to buy clothes, food or even an apartment—they all came free, as did a brand new convertible. By 1950, fans in Montreal, where his NHL playing rights were held, were beginning to tire of the talk of the superstar down the river. Béliveau himself said he could not move to Montreal—first he was loyal to the Quebec fans who idolized him, and second, he was making too much money! For two years, he played a handful of games with Les Canadiens and scored several goals. But he kept on returning to Quebec and the Colisée, and to fans like Aunt Elga, loyally cheering him on.

Finally, the General Manager of the Canadiens, Frank Selke, realized the only way to get Béliveau to Montreal was to do something drastic. First he purchased the entire Quebec Senior League Jean was playing in, to force him to move. Second, in his own words, "I opened the vault and said, take what you like." At one hundred thousand dollars for five years, Jean Béliveau was making four times what most professional hockey players were earning at the time.

But the investment paid off: in 1956, he won the Hart trophy as the best player in hockey and he was chosen the first all-star team centre ten times, including four years in a row. Oh, yes, and from 1956 to 1960, the Montreal Canadiens won the Stanley Cup a record five times in a row. In 1962, he became team captain, replacing Doug Harvey. In the years that followed, he continued to lead the Habs, as they won the Cup again and again: 1965, 1966, 1968 and 1969.

In 1971, running out of steam and diagnosed with a heart that was compared to an Austin Mini engine powering a Rolls Royce, he took his final bow. His numbers were impressive: 507 goals, 712 assists, 1219 points, 2 Hart trophies, and 10 championships. When he retired, he insisted that if the team were to hold a special night for him, all the benefits of the evening would go to charity, expecting a small amount that could be distributed easily, Jean ended up with a three-million-dollar fund that he continued to administer. He came in as a class act, and he went out as one.

All throughout his career, in the cold smoky Colisée or watching on television from her apartment on La Grande Allée in downtown Quebec, my Aunt Elga continued to love Jean Béliveau. But he never knew it.

Then came the winter of 1976.

It was my first time in the Montreal Forum as a reporter. I could not believe my luck. I sat in the press box overlooking the ice and watched the game far below, as what appeared to be ants moved the puck deftly around the ice. I loved rubbing shoulders with the likes of former greats Maurice "The Rocket" Richard, Doug Harvey, Dickie Moore and Henri Richard, and between periods I sat with the other reporters chatting, eating the famous Forum hot dogs (free for us!) and attempting to chat knowledgeably with the journalists who came in and out. Many of them I recognized from television.

After the game, I realized I was going to be allowed into the dressing room to interview the players. I was a bit intimidated, but I did not know what to expect. This was no ordinary dressing room: it was more like a museum describing the history of the Montreal Canadiens. It was, and is, a place so hallowed it has been duplicated in the Hockey Hall of Fame.

As I entered, I spotted a mahogany plaque with the names of the winners of the Vézina trophy for best goaltender, carefully written in yellow paint, with the year each played. (Bill Durnan, Jacques Plante, Charlie Hodge) and as I worked my way into the room there were the players, in various states of undress, talking to reporters. Ken Dryden standing barefoot, at 1 m 90 (6'4"), still very tall. Along the left-hand side, Guy Lafleur, Steve Shutt, Peter Mahovlich, Yvan Cournoyer.

Behind them were more plaques, listing the players on every Canadiens team to have won the Stanley Cup since 1917. On the opposite bench sat the great defencemen: Serge Savard, Guy Lapointe and Larry Robinson all with their long legs stretching into the room. Above them was a huge sign with photos of the Canadiens players who had been inducted in the Hockey Hall of Fame: Aurel Joliat, Newsy Lalonde, Howie Morenz, Doug Harvey, Maurice Richard, Jacques Plante, many others and of course, Jean Béliveau. Below it was the inscription in French and English, "To you, we throw the torch to hold on high."

In the middle of the room stood Scotty Bowman, the Habs' coach, and a very tall man in a suit. The man turned towards me. It was Jean Béliveau. I did not know what to do. I had interviewed Prime Minister Trudeau and Brian Mulroney, but this was different. They were mortals. This was a god.

As it happened there was a rumour that the NHL was going to ask Jean Béliveau to be its next president. I thought to myself, "You are never going to be a reporter if you cannot speak to people who intimidate you." So, knees knocking, I asked Jean Béliveau what he thought of the rumour.

He was a true gentleman, making me feel at ease: he said he did not put much stock in rumours, and was quite content as an executive with the Canadiens. I thanked him and moved on. But from that time on, we would exchange a few words and I would ask a few questions for stories I was working on.

One day I got up the courage to tell him about my Aunt Elga, his greatest fan. I told him "my Aunt lives in Quebec City, is 81 years old and has followed your career ever since you came to Quebec. She is getting older now, but she loves hockey and you are still her favorite player. If you are ever in Kamouraska, if you would drop in for two minutes, she would be happy for the rest of her life."

"Well, Andrew, it happens I am going to Rimouski next summer. I will drop in on her then."

I was stunned, and thrilled. But I did not tell Aunt Elga about it. The anticipation might kill her as would the disappointment if he did not show up.

The next July, I called him at the Forum to make sure he remembered his comment. He said "of course! It is in my date book. I will be there at about 2 p.m. on July 21."

The big day came, and I stood on guard outside the house, Aunt Elga completely unaware of the moment. A long blue Cadillac pulled up, parked at the Hotel Maurice Richard across the road from our house and out stepped a big man wearing sunglasses and holding a partly lit cigar. It was Béliveau. True to form, he stopped to talk to the two very surprised men delivering Molson beer to the hotel. Ever the Molson company man, Le Gros Bill put them at ease by talking about their deliveries, when I came up to him.

We traded small talk about his drive, and I explained that my Aunt Elga had no idea that he was coming, nor did my 89-year-old grandfather.

He walked up the stairs to the front door on the wide verandah and knocked twice with the big iron ram's head doorknocker. I heard my mother call, "Aunt Elga, there is a gentleman at the door for you." She came to the door, looked up at the big man in the sunglasses and was a bit confused. Who was this?Why was he asking for her?

He removed the sunglasses and she could see it was her idol.

"I have been waiting a long time to do this," he said as he bent down to her 5 foot 1 inch frame and kissed her on the cheek.

She was stunned. Too stunned to talk, in fact, except to say, "I cannot believe it! I cannot believe it!"

As le Gros Bill entered, my grandfather got up

from reading the newspaper and gave him a hearty "Bonjour Jean!" to show he was welcome in our house. He stayed and chatted, and we gave him a tour of the old house. Aunt Elga regained her composure and began to chat about the Canadiens, about Quebec City and the old days at the Colisée. My grandfather talked about fishing and hunting, and even about his time as a hockey player in Quebec City, and his cousin who had won the Stanley Cup in the early 1900s. It was like old home week. And then, Jean had to go.

As he walked out with my father, Aunt Elga and me in tow, a young neighbour, Claudine Anctil, was crossing the street with her niece in a stroller. My father gestured "Claudine, viens ici!" She thought he wanted to talk to her, but as she approached, my father said, "Claudine Anctil, je te présente…" and before he could finish, Big Jean had taken off his sunglasses, and Claudine squealed "Jean Béliveau— c'est pas possible!!"

It was quite a moment. They still talk about "The Day Jean Béliveau came to Kamouraska" in the Anctil household.

Before we bid him good-bye, we took a photo of little Aunt Elga and Big Jean Béliveau. For months afterward, the doorman at her apartment in Quebec City would stop perfect strangers to show them the photo of "Mademoiselle LeMesurier" and Jean Béliveau. It was a photo she looked at every day on her dresser, right up until she died in the fall of 1981, soon after her 87th birthday.

About a decade later, I was in the Toronto airport, and there sitting across from me was Jean Béliveau. I went up to him and said, "Jean, you probably don't remember me, but...." He interrupted me: "Yes, I do. You are the journalist with the grandmother—no, the aunt—who has a house in Kamouraska."

"That's right."

"How is she?"

"Well she died a few years ago, and she was very happy. Especially that she had met you."

"I am so sorry. Une belle vielle dame, et une visite memorable."

He said he was flattered that he had done something so simple for her. Then we chatted about the latest hockey news and the abrupt retirement of Guy Lafleur from the Habs the day before. The conversation went on for about half an hour, when they called my plane, and I had to go.

"C'était un grand plaisir de vous revoir," I said. He replied in English, "Yes it has. I hope to talk again soon. And thanks for remembering me."

I paused. I could not believe what he had said. He was thanking *me* for remembering *him.*

Over the years, we saw one another frequently as our paths crossed, in restaurants, at hockey games, and at community events, where he spoke with such wisdom and authority. And each time he was always the same perfect gentleman. A class act.

I could never forget how he stooped down to kiss the cheek of an old spinster, who had loved him so devotedly all her life. That day, when he made my great-aunt so happy she could hardly speak.

The Voice

By Andrew Caddell

Christmas of 1958 was a time of mystery and secrets, and sleeping in fresh sheets in brand new pyjamas wondering if and when Santa Claus might come and visit me at my grandmother's big old house in Montreal.

As people filed in for the annual *réveillon* on Christmas Eve, I could hear the voices drifting in and out of my sleep, until they finally disappeared.

At some point they departed into the snow early in the morning, filled with good wine, Christmas cookies and delicacies like *tourtière* and jellied meat. The next morning, a stocking had magically appeared under my bed. I searched through it to see what special treats might be found inside. An orange, some chocolate, a small book, some socks, and a little batteryless crystal radio.

Of all the presents I received that snowy Christmas morning, I am not exactly sure what my largest or most expensive gift was, but I can recall to this day that one small radio. It was made of red plastic and golden tin, with wires and an earpiece. So simple, yet that gift offered more than any other, because it opened my eyes to the world around me. It was called "The Rocket Radio."

It was the shape of a small missile, about five inches long, an inch in diameter and topped with a golden cap. Attached at one end was a long wire with a pair of small "alligator clips;" at the other end was a thin wire with an earpiece. It had a small circular dial at the top, to receive stations. To operate it, one had to attach it to something metal—preferably a metal radiator, which we had plenty of in our old house—to act as a ground. Once that was done, I would move the little dial back and forth until I found a station. There were not many stations this little radio could receive in the winter of 1958-59. But it did pick up the Montreal station of the Canadian Broadcasting Corporation, the CBC.

And it was thanks to The Rocket that one night I heard The Voice.

That first Saturday after Christmas, I was in bed, fiddling with the little radio. The television coverage of the hockey game did not start in those days until 9:00 p.m.—way past my bedtime. So I had never watched a hockey game on television that I could recall. But this night, hiding under the covers, and in between the "crickle-crackle" of The Rocket's feeble reception, I could make out the description of a Montreal Canadiens game. I wiggled the little rod to pick up the station, then I lost it, then another interrupted. I wove crazily in and out of different music and sounds until I could finally hear it loud and clear:

"Now the Canadiens will have the man advantage for the next two minutes or less.....Toe Blake sends out the formidable combination of Moore, Richard and Béliveau, with Harvey and Johnson the two pillars on defence."

What kind of language was this? "Formidable combination"? "Pillars on defence"? Then the description of the play began.

"Shot on goal ... Plante makes a rapier-like save, and holds on.... Now the face-off to the left of Plante ... Harvey deftly moves the puck ahead to Moore on the left side, Moore waiting, plays it gingerly around the boards, Béliveau waiting. Béliveau negotiating contact with the puck, slips it backwards to Richard, again patiently to Harvey who returns the favour, back to Béliveau, to Richard, They score!!!"

This was magic. Not the radio, but the voice in the radio. This man described a game with word pictures, so that anyone listening could imagine himself or herself in the Montreal Forum that night. Even six-year-old me, my Rocket attached to the radiator at my house.

And there was more.

"Gordie Howe slips by Turner, takes the puck, a cannonading drive, a brilliant stop and the puck ends up in Plante's paraphernalia."

Paraphernalia? Cannonading drive?

Who was this man? Where did he come from? And where did he get these words? I soon found out. All I had to do was ask my older brother, Ian. He knew everything. Plus he got to stay up and watch the hockey game.

"Don't ya know?" he asked with the incredulity that only a nine-year-old can muster over a younger sibling of six. "That's Danny Gallivan, the Voice of the Montreal Canadiens. He is a *legend*."

So now I knew. I could always rely on my brother for the straight goods on the world outside. It was especially the way he said "A *legend*." At six years old, I was introduced to the power of the media. It also made me think I might like to be on the radio too. I was only six years old, but such is the inspiration of *legends*.

Indeed, my brother was right. Danny Gallivan was a *legend*. For more than 30 years he was known as "the English voice of the Montreal Canadiens." He was an important part of being a Canadiens fan, almost as much as the players themselves. I recall the first time I bought hockey cards, and I made the mistake of asking where the "Danny Gallivan" card was. Again my brother set me straight.

"Andy, they don't have cards for the hockey announcers! Only for *the players*." While being dismissive, he sounded a little bit sympathetic, as if it *might* have been a good idea. Especially because Danny Gallivan was a local hero: he lived in our town.

In our little town of 6,000 souls on the edge of Montreal, there was no sign that said "Welcome to Montreal West: home of sports icons," but there could have been: we boasted three icons of Canadian sport: Sam Etcheverry, the greatest CFL quarterback ever, Hector "Toe" Blake, the greatest NHL coach ever, and Danny Gallivan, the greatest broadcaster ever.

When it came to Danny, we always bragged that he lived in our town, but we never saw him.

He was a ghost. Unlike Sam or Toe, we did not see him in the stores, or picking his kids up from school. Then again, how could we? Neither I nor my friends really knew what he looked like. In those days, television never showed hockey announcers on camera. We could only hear their voices. Listening to my little Rocket radio, I could only imagine.

This was a subject of some discussion among the kids at school. How would we know what he looked like? Well, we could listen for The Voice in the local pharmacy or grocery store, maybe hang out on his street. Once I thought I heard him having a coffee at the local restaurant, but when I got closer, he was gone. Worse off, his kids were not our age and didn't go to our school. So we never met him. He was a mystery, as a Voice should be.

He was so important to us as hockey fans, that even though my brother and most of his friends supported any team but the Canadiens (because in those days they always won) we were all agreed: Danny Gallivan was the greatest broadcaster of all time. When the Canadiens played the Leafs, or when the circus was in Montreal and our Habs were not playing at the Forum, or during the playoffs, we were *forced* to listen to Foster Hewitt or worse, his son, Bill. It was an even greater reason to hate the Toronto Maple Leafs. Their broadcasters were awful! Or so we in Montreal believed.

What was worse was that we had been told over and over again by the hated Toronto media that Foster Hewitt was the *best ever*. To give him credit, he had been the first person to ever broadcast a hockey game, and he owned the expression "He shoots, He scores!" But he was long past his prime when I was a kid and could not even pronounce the French names of the Canadiens. Yvan Cournoyer's name, pronounced "Courno-i-ay," came out Coor-noy-err." I think he once called Jean Béliveau *"Gene"*!

Danny Gallivan was different. Not only could he pronounce all the complicated names, mixing "Bay-lee–vau" with Ree-sharhd" and "Jacques Plahnte." And then there were the words he invented or resuscitated. "Paraphernalia," instead of a player's equipment. "Cannonading" instead of the pedestrian "booming." Jean-Guy Talbot did not just turn up ice with the puck, he "wheeled." And as we all recalled in our games of pick-up hockey, Serge Savard's patented turn at the blue line was the "Savardian Spinerama."

There were so many more. Players "anticipated," "observed," and "negotiated contact" with the puck. Listening to a hockey game or watching, was a lesson in vocabulary. And every name was right and every call was simultaneous with the play on the ice.

So, it was clear: Danny Gallivan was not your average hockey broadcaster. A Latin scholar in university, he was genuinely erudite. He thought about the importance of words and descriptions. He never talked down to his audience and he was always as fast as the game itself.

In my neighbourhood, we all knew the details of his life: born in Sydney, Nova Scotia, he began broadcasting at a local radio station in Antigonish, Nova Scotia while attending St. Francis Xavier

University. He taught high school algebra and Latin in Antigonish following graduation, went into the army and then went back to broadcasting. He was in Montreal calling a junior playoff hockey game between a Halifax team and the Montreal juniors when a CBC producer heard him. He filled in for a sick announcer in 1950, and people liked him so much that in 1952, he began a career with Hockey Night in Canada that lasted 32 years, and 1,800 Canadiens games in his career, most of them from the CBC booth high above the ice of the "temple of hockey," the Montreal Forum.

He had a special technique, spotting the players by face and number and memorizing them earlier on game day. Then when game time came, he would lean dangerously (or as he might say, "precipitously") over the edge of the booth to get a closer look, microphone in hand. When the network moved to "headsets" with earphones and mini-mikes combined, he evidently hung on to an unconnected microphone in his hand so that he could still have the feel of his description of the game.

The time finally came when I did meet him. The first time, he was the speaker at a night organized by the local Wolf Cub Packs. The featured attraction was another local hero, Doug Harvey, the all-star defenceman of the Canadiens, who lived in neighbouring Notre-Dame-de-Grace, part of Montreal. But so many of the questions were directed to the host of the evening, Danny Gallivan, that I seem to recall he had to ask us to direct our questions to Mr. Harvey. When it was over I went up to the Voice and Doug Harvey, mumbled a few words, collected a couple of autographs and was gone.

The next time was a benefit a few years later for our church. It seemed that our minister and Danny had known each other growing up in Sydney, Nova Scotia. They told stories about how the minister, Reverend White, was quite a hockey player. A younger Danny lived in his neighbourhood and used to carry his skates to games. They stayed in touch, and by chance, both landed in Montreal.

Because I knew Reverend White pretty well, I asked him to introduce us. I shyly approached him and said how much I wanted to be a broadcaster. He seemed genuinely interested. "Good for you. Keep working at it," said The Voice.

Then suddenly, the passage of time accelerated. I grew a little older if not bigger, and it was long after the hockey season in the hot, hot summer of 1966. A group of us were hanging out at the local tennis club and swimming in our town's brand new public pool. We thought it couldn't get much better than this: we were just discovering girls and going to "teen" parties. I was all of 14, and feeling every bit as awkward as any 14-year-old ever did. A bit of acne here, a bit more uncoordinated than I had been before, playing a lot of tennis, swimming at the pool. And hanging out.

A couple of the kids at the tennis club had friends who sailed on the river near Montreal. There was a portion where it widened and calmed a bit before it tuned into the raging rapids near Lachine. That area was called Lake Saint Louis.

On the other side of the lake, heading towards the US border, was a small town known as Woodlands, which had its own sailing club. And the Woodlands club was where (or so we heard) the action was. So when we got wind of a party over there, we figured we had to find a way to go. So, being a bit ingenious, we hit on the perfect solution: we invited ourselves.

We did have a contact, though: one of the girls we knew from our town went to Woodlands. Her name was Paula. I didn't really know her last name. Who knows other kids' last names at that age? It's Mike and Pete, and Mary and Laurie. Anyhow, Paula was cute and funny, and a year or so younger than me. I didn't think much more about her than that. She was part of our little tennis club group. And we ended up going to the party and hanging out at the Woodlands Sailing Club party.

It was a typically hot Montreal summer night, which is to say it was blisteringly humid and so thick with the scent of rain we thought the clouds would burst any minute. Instead the clouds poured down our faces in sweat, as we danced and danced all night. We were trying to play it very cool, with our neat "Beatle" haircuts hanging over our foreheads and our shirts hanging out of our cut-off jeans. The music was, naturally, Beatles, Beach Boys, the Four Seasons, and Roy Orbison. There were teenagers of all ages, although we were among the younger ones.

My parents, who had some say in this, didn't believe I should stay out beyond midnight, so about 11:30 I started asking for a ride back to town. Soon the dance was over, and I was told we would get a lift with someone's dad. Paula told me she had a lift. So I stuck with her, as we stood outside the old wooden clubhouse.

Eventually, in the dark, a late model sedan pulled up and I jumped into the back seat in the dark. Paula slipped into the front seat. I think my buddy Mike Holding might have joined me in the back.

So, there I was sitting in the back seat of the car, behind the driver. And Paula said, pretty innocently, "Andy, this is my Dad. Dad, Andy."

"Hi, how are ya, Andy?" came the sound. It was The Voice coming out of the dark! That high-pitched whine that sounded like a plane warming up on the runway, or the siren at the Montreal Forum at the beginning of the first period or the end of the third. Except this sound was calling my name. I paused, half in terror, half in sheer astonishment.

Then I remembered. Paula's last name was *Gallivan.*

I tried to sound cooo-oo-l. "Oh, me? Me? Oh, ah, hum, Mister Gallivan... Fine. It was a-a-a-a-a Great dance. Just great."

The Voice continued. "Interesting. So where are you at school?"

"Ahhhh, ummmm, ninth grade—*going into* ninth grade... at Montreal West High..." This was getting difficult. I had to think.

"And are you playing any hockey?"

Now this was a problem. I really didn't play that much hockey. I loved hockey, but ever since my eyes went bad, I only played house league. Perhaps I should lie....no, Paula would turn me in if I did, and I could not lie to The Voice. "Mmmm, well, tennis right now, and this winter, maybe rep if I can make it, maybe house league. I play rugby. And I love football." I was not sure if this was the right thing to say to the Voice.

"Me, too. I go to all the Als (Alouettes) games when I can."

Phew.

The conversation went on for about 20 minutes as we wound over the bridge to Montreal, and to my house. Then Mister Danny Gallivan, Paula (whose name I now knew) and Mike dropped me off at my house. I walked up the path and waved back at them.

I began to think about it over and over: I was still incredulous. The Voice had been talking to me! It was so bizarre: he was talking to me as if from space. I could hear him, but until I got out of the car, I never saw his face. But I could see the back of his head, and hear his voice *talking to me*. To me! I began to feel like one of the early prophets when God spoke to them. But I got to *talk back*.

That was the last time I talked to the Voice for many years. As I grew older, I did become a broadcaster, as I had promised myself when I was younger. As a very junior radio reporter, I would occasionally bump into The Voice at the Canadiens games and remind him of our town connection, and even though neither he nor his family live there any longer, he was still friendly. In a chance encounter in an airport, he remembered me immediately, and introduced me to a friend of his from Newfoundland. And gradually he became Danny to me as much as I was Andy to him. He was no longer either Mister Gallivan or the Voice.

In the summer of 1992, I had been elected a member of our little Town Council, and we decided to hold a special commemoration for a little patch of green space in the north end of the town: it was to be called "Toe Blake Park." As Toe was quite ill, we invited many of his former players from the Canadiens, and we asked his family, his neighbours and friends to come. Jean Béliveau spoke; it was great to see him again. He had a great line: "When you look at all us old players here, you see a lot of white hair. That was because of Toe Blake: he made us afraid to lose." There were dozens of people for the speeches at the park and the small reception afterwards at the Town Hall.

One of the guests was Toe's old neighbour, Danny Gallivan. He was looking a bit frail, and his dark curly hair had turned grey, but at 75, it was not surprising: he had lived an extraordinary life. When he greeted me, that familiar rich whine came out his famous mouth: "Andy, how are ya? So you are on the Town Council? How is that going? What an accomplishment! Do they still hold the Garbage Bowl (our annual New Year's football game) here every year? You know my kids loved that thing. I have so many memories. Isn't it great Toe got a park named after him?!" It all seemed to spill out.

We managed to chat a little bit before and after the ceremony, but I didn't get time to really talk until I walked him out to a friend's car. We stood by the car for a while, then slipped into the back seat, talking about the old times in our town, about his family, but mostly about hockey. We compared the fabulous teams he had seen and all the great players he had covered. I asked him what he thought about hockey in 1992, and said I thought the Canadiens teams in the 1970s were amazing "but of course, that team was not as great as the Habs that won the Cup five times in a row in the fifties," I added.

He surprised me when he said, "Well, those teams dominated, but the game changed so much in 20 years, that 1975 to 1979 team was a power-house." If anyone would know, he would. He called the games for both those teams.

He talked proudly about his children and how accomplished they were, about what they were doing. He asked about their old friends, some of whom I still stayed in touch with. About 45 minutes later, we were still at it, yakking away amiably, with Danny playing the old professor catching up with a long-ago student. The fellow who was driving him was getting impatient. "Danny, we have to go." and so, reluctantly, I slipped from the back seat, and he offered his hand.

"Well, this has been very pleasant, Andy. We should stay in touch and get together again." I nodded in agreement, and hoped it could happen. As he drove off, I stood in the Town Hall parking lot thinking how extraordinary it was that Danny Gallivan, The Voice, *the legend*, was treating me like an old friend. It was a moment to remember.

We never did get together and have that next chat. It was not long after our discussion in the Town Hall parking lot that the news came he had passed away. The tributes poured in, and a service was held at the local parish. The newspapers were overflowing with tributes. The community and his family gave him a great send-off.

The Voice had been stilled: he was gone, but never, ever forgotten. Not by the millions of hockey fans and hockey players for whom he was, in many ways, the symbol of the Canadiens. Not for the Hockey Hall of Fame, where he had been admitted long before. And not to all his friends in our town. Nor to people who never met him, who only knew him as The English Voice of the Montreal Canadiens.

But especially not to that little boy with the "Rocket Radio" under his covers in the winter of 1958. He never forgot The Voice.

The Kid

By Dave Stubbs

Seven-year-old Jack Caddell remembers the pain he felt last September when he learned that Canadiens captain Saku Koivu had cancer.

"In my heart I felt very, very bad," Jack said yesterday, watching the Canadiens breeze through an optional practice at the Molson Centre to prepare for tonight's fourth game in their National

Hockey League playoff series against the Carolina Hurricanes.

"I don't like it when people are sick, and I like it even less when it's Saku."

It was then that the talented, precocious minor-hockey player from Ottawa told his father, Andrew, that he had to do something—anything—to help his hero. "I like Saku because he's small, he's fast and he has really good moves, like me," Jack said yesterday.

Andrew Caddell told his son, "You should pray for Saku to get well. And for every point you score this season, we'll give you $5 that you can give to cancer research."

A nice gesture that wouldn't cost a lot, Caddell must have thought. A year earlier, Jack had scored six goals.

So Jack went out for the Novice C Sandy Hill Flying Mangoes and tore up the league, scoring 29 goals and 10 assists in 23 games. Caddell and his wife, Elaine Feldman, rounded off their contribution at $200, a total that was matched by Jack's grandparents, Phil Caddell and Shirley

Feldman, his aunt, Susan Feldman, and his older brother, James.

Yesterday, the father took his son out of school for a day, and they drove to Montreal with $1,000, a contribution they would make to the Canadian Cancer Society in Koivu's name.

The Canadiens captain's recovery from non-Hodgkin's lymphoma and return to the ice has been one of the most inspiring stories this season.

Yesterday, wearing a knee-length Koivu jersey, Jack was bigger than his 4 feet and 52 pounds when he was ushered into the club's Molson Centre gym, and in strolled the player around whom his hockey universe revolves.

"So there's the man," exclaimed Koivu, exchanging a high-five with his starstruck fan.

"You're a special guy."

Koivu immediately produced one of his game-used sticks as a gift for Jack, who was so dazzled that he insisted a trade be made, leaving one of his own considerably shorter sticks with Koivu. They chatted like long-lost friends, Koivu clearly moved by Jack's fund-raising effort.

"People in this world are doing great things, but we seldom hear about them," said Nicole Mireault, communications director of the Quebec branch of the Canadian Cancer Society. "We think that everybody is bad, selfish, too busy or too stressed to do anything but look after themselves.

"When you look at Jack, you see that's not exactly true."

Andrew Caddell's family was living in Geneva four years ago when a friend presented three-year-old Jack with a red Canadiens sweater. By age 5 he was playing in a league of seven-year-olds, clearly a fine young talent.

Jack had gotten to know hockey through a computer game, memorizing all the numbers and names of the Canadiens he had never seen.

Soon his No. 25 Vincent Damphousse jersey was replaced with a white sweater bearing Koivu's No. 11.

"Basically, the first team I ever knew was the Habs and they're the team I grew up with," Jack said. "People were telling me the Habs were the greatest team of all time."

Living today in hockey-mad Ottawa suggests he should be a fan of the Senators, the Canadiens' opponent in the Eastern Conference final should both teams advance to the next round.

In fact, a Senators executive lives one street over in Ottawa East, and often asks Jack why he's not sporting the red, white and black of the home team.

"We like the Sens," he replies, "but the Habs are legends."

Jack hears little heckling in Grade 2 at École Francojeunesse, the French school he attends that's well stocked with Canadiens fans.

And despite their Ottawa address, his family has a strong Montreal connection: grandfather Phil Caddell was in the Forum in March 1936 for all six overtime periods of the longest game in the history of the NHL, and his great-grandfather, Jack Groper, years ago put Canadiens icon Maurice Richard to work at Albert Oil.

Two seasons ago, Jack was the youngest player in Ottawa's novice-hockey system; this year, he was his team's most valuable player in the Ottawa City tournament.

After a summer of golf, tennis, baseball, soccer and some road hockey, he has next year's production figured: "From six goals to 29 in one year is a five-times increase," he said. "So if I do that again next year, I should score close to 150."

The Canadian Cancer Society later told Jack his donation will go to the National Institute of Cancer of Canada, the society's scientific arm.

But more important to a 7-year-old boy yesterday was basking in the presence of greatness, sitting in the Canadiens gym, rubbing shoulders and comparing sticks with Koivu.

"Nice meeting you," he told Koivu on the way out the door, back to reality. "And I scored 29 goals with that stick. You can use it if you want."

La Patinoire

By Andrew Caddell

It is, quite literally, the *only* game in town.

In Kamouraska, Quebec (population 701) winter hits with a vengeance. The snow rages in off the wide Saint Lawrence River at 60 kilometres per hour and the pastoral scenes of long, hot summers and days at the beach are soon forgotten. Where from June to August there were open fields to run in and wide shores to swim from, there is now only a vast expanse of ice and snow.

From one end of the village to the other—two quick kilometers in a passing car—there is only one colour: white. It envelops the town like a huge ball of cotton; resembling the miniature diorama Christmas villages that you see in department store windows. It reflects the sun, and mirrors the clouds. There are shades of white, from grey-white to blinding light.

And the colder it gets, the more snow there is and the better the ice develops. And in winter, in Quebec, hockey is all about the ice. Because hockey is not just a sport, but a religion in these parts. So, when the cold comes in, anyone with a stick and skates heads to the old courthouse, the *Palais de Justice*, beside which stands the village's one and only rink, known simply as "*La Patinoire*" because there is no other.

Winter in Kamouraska is quiet and peaceful and the winter nights are long. The sun rises just after breakfast and it sets long before dinner time. Aside from television, the occasional visit to the local Bibliothèque or a shopping trip to

116

Rivière-du-Loup half an hour away, there is not a lot to do on a weekend or holiday evening.

Except for hockey, that is. From dawn to dusk and into the night, hockey on the old rink is what you do if you are any kind of able-bodied male or female from six to sixty.

A cold winter in Kamouraska means one thing and one thing only: good ice and an early start to the shinny season. Some winters are measured by the shortness or length of the time the ice stays on the rink. A long winter in Kamouraska can be a good thing.

Around the card tables in the basement of the old Palais du Justice, the veterans of the shinny season have their say.

"Ah, it was a good year last year, " says one 12-year-old, "we had ice on December 1."

"Not so good the year before," adds another. "Just at Christmas. Pourri!" You didn't even have to know that meant "lousy" the way he spat out the word.

The basement of the ornate old Palais de Justice is the hang-out for rink rats of all ages, sizes and shapes. In one corner is the snack bar, run by "*Ti-Vieux*" (the little old man) whose real name was René, but no one called him that: he is *Ti-Vieux* to everyone. In the centre of the room was the card table where the older Anctils—Jean-Guy, Gilles or David—hold court with their friends. In the back some teens are playing pool and a couple of younger kids are warming up while playing video games.

Many years before, I came to Kamouraska in February and spent a day at *la patinoire* with my cousin and some friends. Among the kids we played against was a little boy, about ten years old, who seemed to always be there. The next morning, we saw him again, lacing up his skates. We mentioned that he was getting an early start. Did he spend the entire day at the rink?

No, I come here after breakfast, then I am here from 9:00 to 11:45, then I have lunch, then I come back at midi (noon), then I play until 6:00, then I have dinner, then I come back at 7:00, then I play until 9:00. So no, I am not here for the whole day."

My cousin and I burst out laughing at the unintended humour.

"*Comment est-ce que c'est drôle*?" Why is that so funny, he asked.

We tried to explain that it was clear he was there for a good part of the day. But we admired his determination, and his love for the game. He had the real *amour de hockey,* the purest form of hockey love. He wanted to play for the sake of playing. As do almost all of the boys of winter, at *La Patinoire* and hockey rinks everywhere. I have seen it in the Alps, on cold winter mornings in Calgary, on a frozen Lake Louise.

I once watched two aging superstars, Gordie Howe and Bobby Hull, practice with Gordie's two sons, Marty and Mark, when they all played for the old Hartford Whalers. Bobby and Gordie were in their last year of pro hockey. It was a Saturday afternoon in an old stadium, and it could have been drudgery, but they were having the time of their lives. That was *hockey-love* too.

The moment that I saw it in its purest form was December 27, 2000. The biggest story in all of hockey that day was the return of Mario Lemieux, known to everyone as Mario the Magnificent.

Especially in Kamouraska. Mario Lemieux was returning to professional hockey. Mario had been called "The French Gretzky." He was the heir to the crown of Guy Lafleur, Jean Béliveau and Maurice "the Rocket" Richard. Lemieux was the definition of a superstar: hard-shooting, good-looking graceful, smart, talented and big. In junior hockey he had rewritten the record books, scoring 658 points in only three seasons.

When he entered the pro ranks as the first draft choice overall, he did not stop. Scoring 683 goals in 12 seasons, he led Pittsburgh to two Stanley Cups. He scored the winning goal in the Canada Cup in 1987. And he was always Magnificent. At six foot five and 220 pounds, he was a giant on skates. The stories about him added to the magic: how when he first skated at three years old, his mother left him on the rink in his Montreal neighbourhood of Ville Émard and came back 30 minutes later to find him zipping around as if he had been on skates forever. There were other accounts in later years of how he won games by scoring all the goals.

He was loved everywhere he played. And nowhere more than in the heart of French Canada, in Kamouraska. For Mario counted for more than just team affiliation. If, by some incredible divine-like intervention, he had been plucked from the draft to wear the "sainte flanelle" (the holy vestment) of the Canadiens, he would have been beyond stardom, beyond superstardom. If the NHL was the pantheon, Lemieux was a hockey god. But even playing in the American steel city of Pittsburgh, he was still "un gars de chez nous"—one of us.

Then disaster struck. Mario was diagnosed with cancer. He fought that and miraculously came back to lead his team. But two seasons later, extreme back pain was crippling the giant. And, in 1997, he decided to hang up his skates again. It was a sad day for Mario, a sad day for his hometown Penguins, but an especially sad day in Quebec.

But now, three years later, he was coming back to play. Against the hated Maple Leafs of Toronto. The newspapers reported the comeback for days after the rumours were confirmed on December 8. The Canadian sports channel decided to place one camera exclusively on him all night—a "Mario-cam." The sports headlines became bigger and bigger as the great day approached.

At 7:00 that night after dinner, my six-year-old son, Jack and I put our Montreal Canadiens jerseys over our sweatshirts. It was always Les Canadiens in Kamouraska. Whether summer or winter, the talk was always "how were the Canadiens going to do this year?" (Once at a neighbour's birthday party in July, the main discussion was whether a new trade would help the Habs win the Stanley Cup!)

There had been a time that talk might turn to the Quebec Nordiques, but rarely. And now the Nordiques were long gone to Colorado. The Habs were the traditional team of French Canada, and as Montrealers they were our team. Because they just always had been, they were also Kamouraska's team. On that, down at "la Patinoire," we all agreed.

So as Jack and I put on our long underwear, sweat pants, and sweaters and then grabbed our sticks and skates, we were set. The highway in front of our house was filled with snow, and the wind off the river was blowing it around the streets and fields like one of those crystal ornaments that you shake. It did not look promising for outdoor hockey that night. I cautioned Jack that there might not be much playing of hockey that night. And not because of the snowstorm.

"I imagine most people in town will be watching Mario on TV."

"Why don't we watch him too, then?"

"Well, first of all we don't have a TV in Kamouraska."

"Oh, yeah."

"And second, we can use the skate."

Jack offered an alternative. "Why don't we go over to the Anctils (our neighbours) and watch there?"

Just as I was about to say "Sorry, that is just not an option," we arrived at the rink. The older Anctils, as usual, were at the rink.

Watching TV.

My heart sank. There they were, in the little "clubhouse" under the Palais, about 20 boys of all ages sitting on school chairs and watching the television. Pittsburgh Penguins versus Toronto Maple Leafs. Mario in his debut.

"Viens, les gars!!" said Ti-Vieux.

"Salut, Jack! Salut Andrew! On regarde Mario." (We are watching Mario), said Jean-Guy, Maxim, David, Jean-Christophe and little Gabriel.

Jack was torn: he wanted to watch some TV, given our TV-less status. But he also wanted to play.

A little depressed at the sight, I asked a few of the boys about playing some hockey. "Allons–y! Let's get out there! Hockey night in Canada can wait! "

Silence.

"Ah, Andrew, il y a trop de neige." A few heads nodded. Too much snow, and besides, the game was just beginning. Mario was taking the ice.

I sat down. I sat and watched, and fidgeted. I wanted to play. I figured Jack would too. But I was not going to get any of these Mario-crazed kids away from the TV and the "Mario-cam." I sat and watched, sitting in the basement of the Palais de Justice with Ti-Vieux and Jean-Guy and David and Gabriel and all the rest. With my skates on.

I sat there for about 10 minutes, watching. And so did Jack. I couldn't stand it. Nor eventually could he.

"Come on, Dad, let's play some hockey. This is boring."

I was inspired. But first I had to explain to Jack that with the snow outside, we would not have much to skate on.

"I'll shovel with you," he said.

So we grabbed two shovels at the doorway and headed out. Off to play some hockey, or some form of it, the two of us.

I slid gingerly across the frozen pathway between the Palais basement door and the rink, pushing the snow away as I went. I opened the rink gate, and surveyed the mounds of snow lightly placed across the surface. This was a light snow, from a cold night. It would not be hard to shovel a small square to play some "one on one" with Jack. Luckily, the wind had blown some snow against the boards, leaving clear ice in the near end.

"Five minutes and we will be playing," I promised. We started to shovel and skate, clearing small paths in the snow, and passing back and forth in our miniature rink space at the end boards. As we moved back and forth, a figure emerged from the basement. Someone headed home no doubt.

No, it was little Gabriel, and he had—a shovel! —in his hands. "Puis-je vous aider?" Of course you can help, we said.

Then 14-year-old Jean-Christophe came out and grabbed a shovel, and started to glide to the other end. Pushing the snow away. Then Maxim, then more and more until we had a virtual army patrolling up and down, and pushing the snow to the edges of the boards.

Then the snow stopped falling. So suddenly, the night sky cleared, and the stars appeared before we knew it. We were no longer fighting the elements. And there was more ice showing on the *patinoire* than snow.

Then out came *Ti-Vieux* with the snowblower. The machine made quick work of what remained on the side boards, so there was no need to continue our labours. One by one, only 15 minutes after we began, we picked up our sticks and began to play.

The ice was perfect. Smooth. Hard. Clean. The snow provided it with an extra sheen. The lights seemed brighter and the air clearer than for many years. The puck moved around as if it was oiled. And for the 15 or so players of all shapes and sizes, the result was a game to remember. I can't tell you the score, or even who scored. I don't think that anyone remembers. It was not that kind of a night. For more than two hours, we played and played. From end to end, we skated and shot and cheered our goals. We played for the pure, uncompromising love of the game.

The next morning, the sun shone brilliantly on the fresh snow deposited on the St. Lawrence

River and the farms lined along the shore. It rolled into the village, with the main road covered enough that the old time horse-drawn sleighs could easily have taken passengers from one town to the next.

I know that morning, across little towns like ours, people awoke to the news of Mario Lemieux's return to the NHL, how he had a goal and two assists, and how it seemed as if he had never left. It was a wonderful story about a professional athlete who came back for the love of the game. Many did not even need to read the newspapers or see the replays, as they had seen it already, every minute, and even the "Mario-cam."

And in Kamouraska, Quebec (population 701), there was also talk about Mario, and there was appreciation of his greatness. But for a small group of kids and adults who were lacing up their skates at the little basement space under the old *Palais de Justice*, that was not the most important story of the day.

All we could talk about, all we could think about that sunny morning was the pure *hockey love* we had all felt the night before—on the one, the only, *la seule Patinoire* in our village. And we could not stop smiling. I'm sure if Mario had been there, he would have been smiling too.

The Rink

By Andrew Caddell

It lies beneath every snow-filled Canadian backyard, waiting to be discovered, like a mother lode known only to those with the patience, devotion and knowledge required to find it. It lies not beneath the surface, but upon it. It is of no real value, but it is at one and the same time, priceless. It's not gold, but silver. It can't be held in your hand, yet its memory will remain in your heart for many years. There are days you might curse it, and others you will worship it. There is no way you can ever remain indifferent to it.

It is that great Canadian tradition, the backyard skating rink. Every Canadian boy wishes he had one, and many have. Wayne had one; the Sutter family had a few. I had one in 1963 and a few more forty years later.

From my experience, I will warn you: the backyard rink is not a hobby, it is a vocation, a mini-career, a time-consuming obsession. For the smoothest ice and the longest season requires diligence and devotion. Ask any amateur rink attendant about his craft and an hour later you may be regretting it. Just as they say there are 57 words for the word "snow" in Inuktitut, to a rink lover, there are a hundred ways to describe ice.

There are no half-measures with a good rink. Beginning in the late fall and ending just before spring, you can enjoy ice for 100 days in most Canadian cities. You can, but it's not easy.

My first attempt at making my own rink came when I was 10 years old. I was disappointed when I realized I could never flood a rink with our old outdoor rubber hose, as the pipes would freeze. Then I discovered the sink next to our old hand-wringer washing machine was equipped with a thread similar to the tap outside. It meant I could attach the hose and never have to worry about the cold weather or frozen pipes. Simply trundle it up the stairs of the basement and spray away onto packed ice outside. It was simple.

Or so I thought.

First of all, we didn't have much money. We didn't have a car. We didn't have fancy hockey equipment. We did not even have a modern washing machine. The old wringer washer was so flimsy that my mother caught her hand in it one morning and it crushed her wedding ring and her ring finger at the same time. So, when it came to acquiring a nozzle for my rink, there were clearly other priorities. Either that or my dad thought I was crazy. Undaunted, I pressed ahead.

Beginning one cold day in December, I shovelled our 25 foot by 40 foot back yard. I packed the snow down where I could: I had to avoid the little cherry tree placed awkwardly in the middle of the yard, just off the neighbour's fence. As I shovelled and packed, packed and shovelled, I scrupulously avoided that tree or I would have been in trouble. My mother loved that cherry tree with all her heart. Nothing should come between a boy and his mom, and that cherry tree was one of her few treasures in life. I was not going to tempt fate by building my skating rink around it.

So I continued my work, shovelling and packing just the way I had been told by all the so-called "experts" I had consulted: my brother's 12-year-old friends. The fonts of wisdom and age. "Pack the snow down, pour on the water. It's a cinch." "Use hot water if you have any—it melts the snow and gives you a smoother rink."

I was willing to listen to anyone. What did I know?

So I packed the snow down. I shovelled and packed, but the truth be told, I did not pack the snow down well enough. As I started to spray, the snow began to undulate. In little humps.

I tried to spray more water, but the little mounds became bigger. And when I sprayed more, I realized I had a problem: it was about 20 degrees Fahrenheit, or 10 below zero. Spraying with my finger positioned over the escaping water, I never thought that my index finger might freeze after a few minutes. Which of course, it did.

So, I took to alternating fingers, and when that did not work, I placed my glove over the opening and alternating between fingers. It did not provide for an easy flow. And so the ice began to roll more. To me it made no sense: ice was supposed to be flat, not wavy.

And yet, I was facing a serious problem: an ice rink with hills. At first I tried to skate over them, but when I realized that would not work, I flooded more. And as I flooded more, the water seeped over every area of the rink. Including my mother's beloved cherry tree. Amazingly, the best ice could be found around the cherry tree. So we played around it. Luckily for me, it survived the winter. I am not sure I could have kept my room if that cherry tree had died.

Gradually over time, and many cold nights and days of freezing, the bumps went away. Problem was, I was the only one using the rink. I skated around in a circle, I deked, I shot. I occasionally had a friend over to take shots on me. But then I realized that although we all loved to watch hockey in our neighbourhood, I didn't know many people who actually played! My brother couldn't skate very well, nor could his friends.

But they did play ball hockey.

So, we played without skates, and a ball, which was fine with me. I just wanted to play **something** on my rink, and at least this way, I could play goal with boots on. The first Saturday was a great success. Then at about 4 p.m. it began to get dark. We had no lights. "Game called on account of darkness," yelled Bobby Clarke, one of my brother's smart-aleck friends.

Just then I remembered my father's extension cord and the 100 watt light bulb he used to focus on small items in his workshop. I hooked it up and went to place it—where?—not the neigh-bour's garage roof, not the wall on the back of the house....aha.

The clothes line. It was perfect. We could slide the light back and forth so that it was in the middle of the rink.

The game continued all that night and into the weeks to come.We were pretty popular in our neighbourhood. The only bad side of it was that I continued to freeze my fingers.

Fast forward thirty years. I was invited to my old friend Dugie Ross's for a New Year's Eve party in the suburbs of Montreal. I do not remember much about that dinner, or even the celebration at midnight. What I do recall is his rink.

As soon as I arrived and took off my coat, he brought me to the window. "Look at this Andy!" (now that I had grown up I did not use the childhood nickname, but Dugie still called me Andy—after all, I still called him Dugie). He opened the dining room curtains and there lay the most perfect rink I had ever seen. It had foot-high wooden boards, smooth as silk ice, and at centre was painted the Big "CH" of the Montreal Canadiens. The ice surface was enormous: 25 feet by about 60 feet. Dugie's whole back yard. Now I could see why I was invited to dinner.

"What do you think?" Dugie said with obvious pride.

"How did you get it so smooth?" I asked

"Plastic!"

"Plastic?"

"Yeah, you lay thick plastic sheeting on the ground, lay down the boards, sealing the breaks to the ground and fill it up. The water freezes evenly— and really quick. We've had ice since early December. "

I was in awe, and I remembered. The secret was plastic.

A few years later, family in tow, we moved to Geneva, Switzerland, which has the same climate as Vancouver: warm and mushy. But cold in the mountains. And in the mountains there was a natural ice rink. My son, Jack, loved that rink. So when we visited his cousin in Ottawa in February one year, he could not believe that Ben had his own private rink in his back yard.

"A lot of Canadian kids have rinks. Wayne Gretzky had one. And so did I." I told him, forgetting that kids remember a lot of things. And also forgetting that adults don't recall what they should about what they did as kids. My humpy rink, for example.

"Can we have one when we return, Dad?"

"Oh, sure, Jack."

So when we came back to Canada five years later, one of the conditions of return was that I build a rink. I thought of Dugie's words of wisdom: *plastic.*

When the first frost hit, I was inspired. I went to the local hardware store and bought heavy-weight plastic sheeting, enough to cover more than 1200 square feet of lawn. As it got colder, I laid out the plastic, placing it from one end of the fenced in yard to the other, placing firewood on it to hold the plastic down. I thought I would start simple: boards and paint could be for another year. But this time I had enough money to buy a proper nozzle, to keep my fingers from freezing.

I pulled out the hose, hooked it up to the outside pipe, and waited. No water. The pipes were frozen. This really was *déja vu*. I hauled out a blowtorch and lit the pipe. It unfroze. And then I stood with the hose, spraying over the endless plastic. I stood and watered, I watered and I stood. This was taking a lo-o-ong time.

I knew I had two problems. The first was frozen pipes. The second was time. I did not have enough of it. I checked the downstairs sink and sure enough, it fit the hose. Snaking it through my basement window, it was long enough to extend right into the back yard. Then I hauled the sprinkler out of the summer shed, and attached it to the other end.

I watched as the sprinkler went from side to side, in a lovely arc, efficiently spreading the water across the plastic. This was wonderful. I could leave the sprinkler on all afternoon, and I might have ice in a couple of days.

I had forgotten about the trees.

The tree branches hung over the yard, not low, but high enough so that the moisture from the spray from the sprinkler stuck on to the branches, which began to freeze, then droop and freeze some more, until I discovered tree branches hanging only a few inches above the surface. And little bits of broken branches scattered across the rink.

Clearly this was not going to work. I needed a sprinkler that went in circles, low to the ground, and not back and forth into the trees. I went back to the hardware store and asked if they had a sprinkler.

"A sprinkler?" the salesperson asked incredulously. "In – November?" She seemed to stretch out the word to make me feel more foolish.

I had to defend myself. I was not a nutcase.

"It is for my rink." She rolled her eyes, sort of saying, "Oh, another one of them."

"Well, let's see."

They had hoses, they had nozzles, but they were clean out of sprinklers. It was the same story all over town.

I went back, broke a few more tree branches off, and began to flood my rink. A few hours later, something was emerging. It looked like a rink, it slid like a rink. There was ice. And aside from the odd cracking plastic underfoot, it really *felt* like a hockey rink.

That night, I continued the flooding, realizing that I was missing something. Lights. But we had no clothesline to place a light on.

I called the electrician: "What would it cost to hook up a 500 watt spotlight from a tree or the top of our kitchen for my hockey rink?"

"About three hundred dollars, at least." My heart sank. Then he came up with a great idea.

"Why don't you get some old Christmas lights and string them around the yard? It doesn't cost much and you will get more light than a 500-watt spotlight.

I did and it was perfect. Some of the lights even blinked.

Two days later, my son Jack and his friend Kai played on the rink for the very first time. There was no snow around, but the temperature was way below freezing.

There was one more obstacle: the pieces of firewood to hold down the plastic had been frozen hard, and many resembled petrified wood. A few minutes with an axe, and the wood was surgically removed.

It was my first day of my first rink. It was December 4.

Many people who have had backyard rinks rave about the chance to meditate while watering the rink in the cold late night air. There are accounts of the joys of standing with a hot coffee and a cigar at midnight in winter. I had neither the hot coffee nor the stogie, but I did not realize how right they were until I got hooked on the habit myself.

There is a special calm on a cold winter's night that only Nordic people, like Canadians, can appreciate. As the water floods out, freezing sometimes on contact, or in even colder nights, as it leaves the hose, the surface shimmers with the steam rising above the rink, and reflects the lights above the haze. On nights like those, I could not help but admire my artistry. The rink, filled with water, finding its own level, and smooth as a baby's bottom. I wanted to grab my skates and take a turn around in the midnight air.

That always had to wait until the return home the next day, when both Emily and Jack were already out on the rink, fighting over whose turn it was. Emily loved her figure skating and Jack wanted to play hockey, and the two did not mix. So we organized 30-minute periods, lasting until well after dinner. Some nights, we had two children at the dinner table, wearing skates. It was the winter equivalent of a backyard swimming pool. When friends came to visit, we would draw them to the kitchen window to look out and see the skating performances or the hockey exhibitions from the warmth of the kitchen.

Then one day, Emily asked if she could have music to accompany her skating, to practice her routines. It is pretty hard to be a figure skater without music, so I went out and bought small outdoor speakers and hooked them up to the stereo. This was a great success with both the children, as Jack would play "The Good Old Hockey Game" and other arena music while out on the rink and Emily would have her skating waltzes and performance music. I was a little wary about any comments from the neighbours, but the selections were always tasteful.

One weekend, she and a friend were rehearsing for a pairs competition, to the old rock and roll song "Stupid Cupid." The lyrics are pretty simple.

Stupid Cupid you're a real mean guy.
I'd like to clip your wings off so you can't fly.
I am in love and it's crying shame & I know that
you're the one to blame!
Hey, hey, set me free.
Stupid Cupid, stop picking on me.

Of course they had to practice it over and over again to get the routine right, and I did not want to keep on pushing the "Start" button over and over, so I simply pushed "Replay." An hour later it was still going, and going. The girls were having a great time, but I think the 30 or so repetitions of the same song might have been a little annoying.

However, there were no complaints from the neighbours, no arrests of indulgent Dads, and the girls won a gold medal the next week.

For Jack, the best part of having his own rink was deking and shooting. As Walter Gretzky had done, I set up coffee cans with water in them, as pylons for deking. So for hours on end, Jack would go back and forth, back and forth, deking and moving.

We also set up a little shooting range for him, against the back yard metal shed. At 6, he could not do much damage, but as he got older, the puck began to make serious dents, so that the shed now looked like the other side of the moon, with little pockmarks everywhere.

The rink was also a magnet for school friends and hockey pals. There were often 4-on-4 games of hockey on the weekend, with squeals of delight and the inevitable arena music resounding from the yard, and with the lights on, going to all hours, One New Year's Eve was celebrated by about a dozen children. One visitor to our neighbourhood from southern Ontario heard the music and asked to join in. He had never played on a backyard rink. He kept on saying "this is incredible!"

The rink gave us some notoriety in the neighbourhood. One night in January, I received a panicked call from one acquaintance, Ed, a prominent Canadian journalist. His ten-year-old had promised his pals they would play hockey on his backyard rink for his birthday party. Problem was, he did not yet have a rink. The birthday was coming up fast and a rink was needed pronto.

Ed asked me to come over and assess what was required. He greeted me at the front door and quickly took me out to the back. He held up a large piece of plastic sheeting. "INSTANT ICE RINK" It proclaimed. I was sceptical.

"What the heck is that?"

"You add water to the bag, set it down overnight and you have a rink."

"Just how big is it?"

"12 feet by 10 feet. 120 square feet."

"Not very big."

"Big enough for Joshua and his friends."

"Hmmm…"

I thought about my own rink: 25 feet by 40, and it was hardly big enough. This plastic bag thing was postage stamp size. Still I did not want to dispel his interest, or make him pessimistic. So I offered to build a real rink with him. We could lay down plastic. Spray for a couple of nights, and suddenly a rink would emerge. He was non-committal, even a bit doubtful.

I thought I would apply some psychology, some positive thinking. Ed had grown up near me in Montréal, and he had travelled the world, so I figured he had the same sort of experiences.

"It is just like French, Ed. You don't realize you are bilingual until you start understanding it on the street, or dreaming in French. And then you know. Same thing with the ice. One night it is just hard snow, and all of a sudden, a rink emerges. It is subtle but sudden. You just have to be patient."

Ed paused. He looked at me, and at the big plastic bag on the ground. He hesitated. Then he said, with a painful expression on his face, "There is only one problem with that analogy. I never learned how to speak French."

Then I knew we were in trouble.

In the end, Joshua celebrated his birthday at a local public rink and a year later, Ed moved to snowless Toronto.

I should not make it sound as if it was always a picnic. It does snow frequently in Ottawa, and after a major snowfall, removing a thousand cubic feet of snow was no joy. But it got done, most times without a snow blower. That would be too easy.

Of course, the driveway and the path were rarely shovelled, but that was not my main priority. Besides, when you clean a driveway or a path, it does not shimmer. And I was not allowed to flood the driveway to extend the rink.

I can only recall the good things about the rink, but all good things must end, they say. As they grew older, Jack and Emily got too big for the surface. Their longer legs only needed three strides from one end to the other. We looked at buying another house, but none had the back yard for a bigger rink, so we stayed where we were. Real estate agents found it frustrating, trying to find the "right" backyard before they found the right house.

So, this year, there is no rink, only a yard filled with snow and memories. I look out to the Christmas tree lights hanging at all angles across the backyard, and see the ghosts of Christmases and New Year's past roaring about. I see the coffee-can pylons lined up for quick shooting drills, and I hear the squeals of excited eight-year-olds. The sounds echo through my mind. But when I look out, there is only snow.

When Michelangelo crafted his masterpiece, David, from a block of granite, he is reported to have said that the statue was "waiting for him" inside the block of stone, and he simply discovered it. That is how I feel about my rink. It lies buried beneath the snow. I know that it's there and, if I were to seek it out, it would reappear.

But for now, it sleeps.

ABOUT THE AUTHORS

Andrew Caddell has been a reporter and broad-caster in Montreal, Ottawa, Calgary, St. John's and Geneva, Switzerland and has been published in several Canadian newspapers. He has also worked for the UN in Europe and Asia and for the Government of Canada. He lives in Ottawa and Kamouraska, Quebec. He plays old-timers' hockey twice a week, and is a sometime goaltender.

Dave Stubbs is a columnist/sports feature writer with the Montreal Gazette. He has been a sportswriter since 1976. Stubbs kept thick hockey scrapbooks filled with game summaries and Red Fisher's Montreal Star stories, collected dozens of Bee Hive Corn Syrup photos and put a fortune of hockey cards through the spokes of his bikes. His fantasy is to travel back in time to the 1950s and watch the great Canadiens dynasty that won five consecutive Stanley Cups. Or a decade earlier, to watch Elmer Lach centre Rocket Richard and Toe Blake on the fearsome Punch Line. Until then, Stubbs is happy to tell the stories of the men behind the game, profiling the superstars of yesterday and today.

Philip "Pip" Caddell (1913-2004) was a wonderful storyteller. While he never played hockey, he loved the game. Born in Canada and raised in Scotland, he returned to this country as a teenaged immigrant. He enlisted for the Second World War in 1939, served in combat with the Royal Canadian Artillery and was promoted to Captain in the field. After the war, he worked as a brewmaster and personnel manager, and worked in dozens of community organizations. Philip Caddell was a proud Canadian until the day he died. And for him, hockey was synonymous with his nationality.

ACKNOWLEDGEMENTS

I wish to acknowledge with great gratitude:

Denise Chong, for her editing suggestions, encouragement and inspiration to keep on pressing to publication.

John Mahoney, photographer extraordinaire for several publications in Montreal over the years, who gave his permission for the photos of Philip and Jack Caddell.

My old friends Dugie Ross, Dane Baily and Steven Johnson, for encouraging me to put these stories on paper.

Ian Shaw, for his tireless encouragement, perpetual optimism, tact, diplomacy and incredible management skills. Ania Szneps, for her superb and precise proofreading. And Caroline Vu, Roger Smith and Elaine Feldman for their editing expertise.

For everyone I played old-timers hockey with and against over the years, in pickup games, shinny and organized leagues in Kamouraska, Montreal, Calgary, Ottawa and Geneva. For the boys and girls on Le Team, The Dips with Sticks and Les Papys. For all the hockey parents who came out early mornings and sat in countless cold arenas, travelled to endless tournaments, and cheered their kids on every game.

Andrew Caddell

ABOUT DEUX VOILIERS PUBLISHING

Organized as a writers-plus collective, Deux Voiliers Publishing is a new generation publisher. We focus on emerging Canadian writers. The art of creating new fiction is our driving force.

Other Works of Fiction published by Deux Voiliers Publishing

Soldier, Lily, Peace and Pearls by Con Cú (Literary Fiction 2012)

Kirk's Landing by Mike Young (Crime/Adventure 2014)

Sumer Lovin' by Nicole Chardenet (Humour/Fantasy 2013)

Last of the Ninth by Stephen L. Bennett (Historical Fiction 2012)

Marching to Byzantium by Brendan Ray (Historical Fiction 2012)

Tales of Other Worlds by Chris Turner (Fantasy/Sci-Fiction 2012)

Romulus by Fernand Hibbert and translated by Matthew Robertshaw (Historical Fiction/English Translation 2014)

Bidong by Paul Duong (Literary Fiction 2012)

Zaidie and Ferdele by Carol Katz (Children's Fiction 2012)

Palawan Story by Caroline Vu (Literary Fiction 2014)

Cycling to Asylum by Su J. Sokol (Speculative Fiction 2014)

Stage Business by Gerry Fostaty (Crime 2014)

Stark Nakid by Sean McGinnis (Crime/Humour 2014)

Twisted Reasons by Geza Tatrallyay (Crime Thriller 2014)

Four Stones by Norman Hall (Canadian Spy Thriller 2015)

Nothing to Hide by Nick Simon (Dystopian Fiction 2015)

Frack Off by Jason Lawson (Humour/Political Satire 2015)

Wall of Dust by Timothy Niedermann (Literary Fiction 2015)

Please visit our website for ordering information
www.deuxvoilierspublishing.com